SPRING HARVEST 2013

THEME GUIDE

YOUR ESSENTIAL GUIDE TO THE SOURCE

COMPILED BY
GERARD KELLY

With contributions from:

Dave Bookless, Melanie Cave, Alan Charter, Kate Coleman, Baroness Caroline Cox, Joel Edwards, Roger Ellis, Martin Goldsmith, Pete Greig, James Hamilton, Jessie Joe Jacobs, Arfon Jones, Bekah Legg, Virginia Luckett, El McKenney, Kay Morgan-Gurr, Cris Rogers, Greg Valerio and Ruth Valerio.

CW00524994

HOW TO USE
THE THEME
GUIDE

This Theme Guide is designed to resource your journey through the Spring Harvest 2013 theme, whether you are making that journey with our teaching team or afterwards in your own local context. The guide takes you deeper into The Source, and discusses what it means to encounter Jesus today.

Each section covers one day of Spring Harvest and explores what impact our encounter with Jesus has on how we live out the gospel; in all we are, say and do. Throughout the guide we focus on the practical response to the truths we discover when asking the question "who is Jesus?"

Through providing background material and suggestions for discussion, further exploration and application, the guide takes us on a journey from being simply spectators in His kingdom, to being participants in His work here on earth.

We pray that as you explore this important theme with us, you will know the presence and power of the God who sent his only Son, so that we may live life in its fullness.

Spring Harvest wishes to acknowledge and thank the following people for their help in the compilation and production of this theme guide.

Steph Adam, Wendy Beech-Ward, Vicky Beeching, Rebecca Bowater, Pete Broadbent, Graeme Bunn, Jaqs Graham, Abby Guinness, Ian Macdowell, Alice O'Kane, Phil Loose, Patrick Regan, Mark Steel, Ruth Valerio, Laura West and Paul Weston.

INTRODUCTION:
THE SOURCE

Say Jesus and people either get happy, or they get mad. They either smile, or a cloud comes over their faces. They are either elated or irritated. Embarrassed, they try to pursue deeper conversation and connection. No other name has such potency. Not Clinton, not Gandhi, not Thatcher, not Lennon.
Carolyn Weber[1]

In Matthew Chapter 16[2] a conversation is recorded between Jesus and his disciples. He asks what it is that people have been saying about him in the towns and villages they have passed through, teaching and healing. 'Some say John the Baptist,' the disciples reply, 'Others say Elijah; and still others, Jeremiah or one of the prophets.'

'What about you?' he asks, 'Who do you say I am?' It is Peter who replies on behalf of the group. 'You are the Messiah,' he says, 'The Son of the living God.'

Jesus responds by honouring Peter, saying that this is not a truth he has merely arrived at by human reasoning, but is a revelation, given to him by the Father. And he goes on to talk about the foundations of the church that he will build. Faith; the church; the movement that will come to be called 'Christian,' will be founded on the rock of this revelation. We are the church when we know who Jesus is. 'The whole story of the world - and of how we fit into it,' Tim Keller writes, 'is most clearly understood through a careful, direct look at the story of Jesus.'[3]

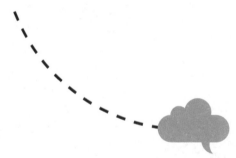

1   Carolyn Weber, Surprised by Oxford: A Memoir, Nashville: Thomas Nelson, 2011

2   Matthew 16:13-20

3   Tim Keller, King's Cross - The Story of the World in the Life of Jesus, New York: Dutton, 2011

WHO DO YOU SAY I AM?

It is tempting to assume that this was a question only for the disciples; that Jesus was testing them, to see if they had yet discerned his true identity. It is tempting to think that today, with 2,000 years of theology and doctrine behind us, the question no longer matters: that today we know who Jesus is. But do we? Really? Or is it possible that our twenty centuries of thinking and writing; of discussing doctrine; of killing each other when we couldn't agree, have done as much to distance us from the revelation of who Jesus is as to bring us closer? Do we need to revisit the question: to hear Jesus asking us, today, as if for the first time, 'Who do you say I am?'

The Source is a response to this challenge. 'The gospel,' the good news of salvation announced in Christ, finds its source in Jesus himself. It is in who Jesus was, in the words he uses to declare the kingdom and the actions by which he proclaims it, that the good news can be found. Can we re-visit this source; stripping away some of our assumptions and presumptions to look again at Jesus? Can we find, in encountering him, what it takes for us in turn to embody good news: in all we are, in all we say and in all we do?

OUR JOURNEY THROUGH THESE QUESTIONS
WILL CONSIST OF FOUR STAGES.

1. The Source will take us back to Jesus. We will look at Jesus in the Gospels; at his words and works and the things he said about himself. We will find that he was, and is, good news in every sense. And we will explore the bigger picture: the process by which the first Christians came to understand that Jesus is indeed God, and what it means that Jesus is the saviour not of humanity alone, but of the universe itself. He is the source of our gospel, but he is the source, also, of all that is.

2. BE will explore what this good news has to say about who we are and where we are. We will explore the twin challenges of being present to God and present to the world. What does the life of Jesus tell me about who I am? How does it challenge me to live where I am?

3. SAY will consider the words we use to explain and proclaim this good news. What do we say, personally, when others ask us what we believe about Jesus and why? Is 'faith sharing' a thing of the past, or are there fresh, new ways to engage in conversation with our peers? And what of our public proclamation; our preaching and writing and cultural engagement? We will ask what we have to say as a church, and what it is that people hear. What does it sound like to be a good news people?

4. DO will turn to action, and ask how it is that we can embody good news in all we do. We will ask what it means to have a practical faith; motivated by love and living the lifestyle of Jesus. And we will explore how we can be a prophetic people, taking actions in the here and now that point to the coming kingdom of Jesus. What are the issues, personally, locally and globally, that are waiting even now for our practical and prophetic action?

In all these areas we will be guided by two goals.

- We want to come to a deeper understanding of who Jesus is, and how it is that he makes all the difference.

- And we want to discover tools and resources that enable us to respond.

To re-visit the source of the good news, it is not enough to simply go back in time – though there is that aspect to our journey. More than that, though, we want to encounter Jesus today: in the here and now of our lives. The words that have come down to us from the past may motivate us to follow Jesus, but it is the encounter with him today that empowers us. We don't simply want to know about the source. We want to be connected. We want to meet him.

As Tim Keller says in King's Cross - The Story of the World in the Life of Jesus, we hope 'that you will find the figure of Jesus worthy of your attention: unpredictable yet reliable, gentle yet powerful, authoritative yet humble, human yet divine. (We) urge you to seriously consider the significance of his life in your own.'[4]

4   Tim Keller, King's Cross - The Story of the World in the Life of Jesus, New York: Dutton, 2011

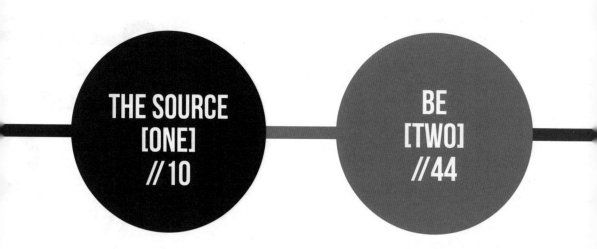

THE SOURCE
[ONE]
//10

BE
[TWO]
//44

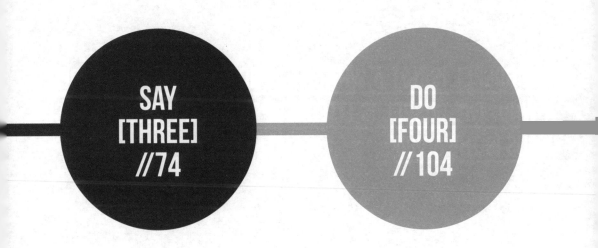

SAY
[THREE]
//74

DO
[FOUR]
//104

THE GOSPEL IS NOT A WHAT. IT IS NOT A HOW. THE GOSPEL IS A WHO. THE GOSPEL IS LITERALLY THE GOOD NEWS OF JESUS. JESUS IS THE GOSPEL.

Carl Medearis

THE SOURCE

[ONE]

THE SOURCE CODE

Right at the start, before anything had happened,
When nothing that would be made had yet
been made,
There was a source code for everything.
The source code was the maker's way of
making things,
Because it was what he himself was made of.
Each thing and everything made by the maker
Has the source code at its centre.
Every ingredient, every invention;
Every part and particle;
Marked; stamped; infused with that which
makes life possible
Later, after the making of many things,
A quite remarkable thing happened.
It was a singularity, a one-off:
The source code of everything became
A specific something.
He entered into life;
Pushed out legs;
Took on a body and a beard;
Became human.
He was as human
As every human born before him,
But unlike any human ever born.
He was a straight line in a world of twists
and turns;
A resounding YES to the second chance,
Against a chorus of condemning cries.
The source code walked the world
Whose fabric he himself had woven.

The one who made us became one of us,
And we saw that the maker's mark was on him.
Something shone from him that shook us all.
He sounded out a note so clear and true
That it is sounding still,
And the very noise of hell can't drown it out.
A man called John was sent to us
With a message from the maker -
To tell the world that the answer so long
waited for was coming.
'I myself am not the answer,' he told us,
'But I am here to tell you that the answer has
been sent.'
He knew that after him the maker's one
true answer would arrive.
'Beside him I am nothing,' he said,
'Compared to the answer that is coming
I am not even a question worth asking.'

The true answer was spoken
When the source code walked among us.
We should have known him;
We should have recognised the maker in
our midst,
But we were blind.
Only a few saw him for who he was:
And those few, though dead, are celebrating still.

So the source code came to us -
Born as one of us;
Walking with us.
'And it is from this very code that life has come
to us,' John said:
'Life upon life, blessing upon blessing, cascading
down to us.'[6]

6   John 1:1-8 Free translation c. G Kelly, 2012

//

Jesus is not only the source of the good news; He is the source of everything! John's prologue 'locates' Jesus in two spheres at once. He is both the cosmic Christ, maker and ruler of all things, and he is Jesus of Nazareth, who came to a specific place and time to announce God's kingdom. We cannot do justice to the question 'Who is Jesus?' unless we take account of both these assertions.

We find the source in history, in the actual events of the life, death and resurrection of Jesus. We look to Jesus in the Gospels to show us the meaning of God's good news.

But we also find the source in eternity, by locating Jesus in the wider story of God. We look to Jesus, the Cosmic Christ, to show us how the plans of God, established before the beginning of time and the promises that will carry us beyond its end, find their focus in this same good news.

To begin to explore this breath-taking good news story, we will explore two vital aspects of biblical faith:

- Firstly, we will look at Jesus in the Gospels. What did Jesus say and do? Who did he think he was? How do his words and actions embody the good news of God? What does it mean for us, today, to build our lives on Jesus as the source?

- Secondly, we will look at Jesus in the story of God. How does the earthly work of Christ fit into the wider narrative of God's plans for his creation? How did the New Testament writers come to see that Jesus was not only the source of the gospel message, but of life itself? What might it look like for us, today, to acknowledge Jesus as the source of everything?

The single biggest, and really one-and-only idea dominating the Gospels is this: the Gospels are about Jesus, they tell the story of Jesus, and everything in them is about Jesus.

SOURCE TEXTS: JESUS IN THE GOSPELS

'The single biggest, and really one-and-only idea dominating the Gospels is this: the Gospels are about Jesus, they tell the story of Jesus, and everything in them is about Jesus.' Scot McKnight[6]

In his book Simply Jesus, Tom Wright explores the challenge of finding 'the gospel in the Gospels'. He remembers being taught a great deal about 'The gospel' - God's plan to rescue humanity through the sacrifice of Christ - but then discovering that the details of this plan were to be found more in the letters of Paul and others than in the four Gospels of Matthew, Mark, Luke and John. And yet these Gospels, and the events they record, are without doubt the foundation of the gospel story. Is there a danger in contemporary expressions of our faith that we rely more on what has been said about Jesus than on what Jesus said? Can we recover the deep and unbreakable connection that the New Testament writers themselves clearly acknowledged between the life, death and resurrection of Jesus and the things they later came to understand about him? Can we get back to Jesus as the source of our faith?
'As far as they were concerned,' Wright says of the four Gospel writers, 'the story of Jesus was the unique turning point of all history.'[7]

Wright explains how it was that in the English language we began to speak of 'the gospel' as something distinct and separate from 'the Gospels': When C S Lewis wrote his famous History of English Literature in the Sixteenth Century, he naturally included a section on the writers of the English Reformation, not least the great translator William Tyndale. Writing for a non-theological audience, Lewis had to explain one point that had obviously

puzzled other readers. When William Tyndale, one of England's earliest Protestants, a disciple of Martin Luther, wrote about 'the gospel,' he didn't mean 'the Gospels' - Matthew, Mark, Luke and John. He meant 'the gospel' in the sense of the message: the good news that, because of Jesus' death alone, your sins can be forgiven, and all you have to do is believe it, rather than trying to impress God with doing 'good works'. 'The gospel' in this sense is what the early Reformers believed they had found in Paul's letters, particularly Romans and Galatians, and more particularly Romans 3 and Galatians 2-3.[8]

The importance of this piece of history is that it explains to us how it has become possible for us to describe 'the gospel' in terms that might bear little reference to the life of Jesus himself, and never quote his own words. Worse still, we can even take large sections of the Gospels and complain that they don't communicate 'the gospel' at all. The solution is not to set Paul against Jesus as if 'the gospel' is somehow a corruption of, or addition to, 'the Gospels'. It is, rather, to rediscover the intimate link between the two: to understand that everything the apostles believed and sought to communicate was built on and derived from the life, the identity, the words and the actions of Jesus. Whoever they thought Jesus was - indeed whoever Jesus himself thought he was - the result was the remarkable explosion of life and faith we call the church, and it was built entirely and unequivocally in his honour.

Considering the location of this problem is essentially in the Reformed/Protestant wing of the church, help has been offered recently from a surprising quarter. Cardinal Joseph Ratzinger, now Pope Benedict XVI, is an accomplished theologian in his own right, and has written extensively on the person and work of Jesus. His book, Jesus of Nazareth, published in 2007, is the result of decades of reading and study. In it he insists on the Jesus of the Gospels not only as a 'historically plausible and convincing figure' but also as the undisputed source of Paul's gospel of grace:

6   Scot McKnight, The King Jesus Gospel: The Original Good News Revisited, Grand Rapids: Zondervan, 2011

7   Tom Wright, How God Became King: Getting to the Heart of the Gospels, London: SPCK, 2012

8   Tom Wright, How God Became King: Getting to the Heart of the Gospels, London: SPCK, 2012

'Unless there had been something extraordinary in what happened, unless the person and the words of Jesus radically surpassed the hopes and expectations of the time, there is no way to explain why he was crucified or why he made such an impact. As early as twenty or so years after Jesus' death, the great Christ-hymn of the letter to the Philippians (cf Philippians 2:6-11) offers us a fully developed Christology stating that Jesus was equal to God, but emptied himself, became man, and humbled himself to die on the cross, and that to him now belongs the worship of all creation, the adoration that God, through the Prophet Isaiah, said was due to him alone (cf Isaiah 45:23).

Critical scholarship rightly asks the question: What happened during those twenty years after Jesus' crucifixion? Where did this Christology come from? To say that it is the fruit of anonymous collective formulations, whose authorship we seek to discover, does not actually explain anything. How could these unknown groups be so creative? How were they so persuasive and how did they manage to prevail? Isn't it more logical, even historically speaking, to assume that the greatness came at the beginning, and that the figure of Jesus really did explode all existing categories and could only be understood in the light of the mystery of God?'[9]

From the other side of the Reformational divide, Scot McKnight endorses this unbreakable connection between the gospel of the apostles and 'the Gospels':

'Let this be said over and over: the apostolic gospel was framed in such a way that the story was centred on and revolved around Jesus. The gospel was (and is) to declare the royal truth about Jesus. Jesus was (and is) the gospel.'[10]

Jesus himself, then, is the source of 'the gospel'. His words. His actions. His identity. Important words are written about Jesus in the New Testament, many of them by Peter, Paul and the other apostles, but it is Jesus they are writing about, and it is Jesus himself who is the heart of the message. 'The gospel' truly is to found in 'the Gospels' because the gospel is Jesus. 'The closer you get to the centre of the gospel, the clearer becomes the very face of Jesus.'[11]

The authors of the New Testament letters took this dynamic link for granted. When they speak of 'the mystery of the gospel' in Romans 16:25 or Ephesians 3:5 & 6, it always relates back to the person of Jesus Christ. When Paul commends Timothy to guard the 'deposit' or 'treasure' of the gospel in 2 Timothy 1:14, he's not just talking about a commodity, but about the grace brought through the appearing of Jesus Christ. We talk about the gospel as a thing at our peril, because we run the risk of being peddlers of a product, rather than ambassadors for a person.

Might there be a need, in our day, to reconnect our understanding of 'the gospel' with our reading of 'the Gospels': to rediscover in who Jesus was, in what he said and what he did, just what the good news, the evangel, really is? A number of writers in Protestant/Evangelical circles have issued just such a challenge in recent years. 'My plea,' says Scot McKnight, 'is that we go back to the New Testament to discover all over again what the Jesus gospel is and that by embracing it we become true evangelicals. We are in need of going back to the Bible to discover the gospel culture all over again and making that gospel culture the centre of the church.'[12]

This, Brennan Manning insists, is the very heart of our faith. 'I believe that Christianity happens,' he writes, 'when men and women experience the reckless, raging confidence that comes from knowing the God of Jesus Christ.'[13]

9   Joseph Ratzinger, Pope Benedict XVI, translated from the German by Adrian J Walker, Jesus of Nazareth, Doubleday, 2007

10   Scot McKnight, The King Jesus Gospel: The Original Good News Revisited, Grand Rapids: Zondervan, 2011

11   Scot McKnight, The King Jesus Gospel: The Original Good News Revisited, Grand Rapids: Zondervan, 2011

12   Scot McKnight, The King Jesus Gospel: The Original Good News Revisited, Grand Rapids: Zondervan, 2011

13   Brennan Manning, The Furious Longing of God, Colorado Springs: David C Cook, 2009

Here are some of the questions we might need to explore if we are to take up this important challenge

Who did Jesus himself say he was? What was his own sense of vocation and purpose? How did later New Testament writers sum up the meaning and purpose of Christ's coming? For a discussion-starter list of Jesus' statements about himself, see www.believers.org/whodid.htm

How does Jesus' sense of self-identity, combined with his words and actions, constitute good news?

How does our contemporary understanding of the good news hold up against this portrait of Jesus? Are we truly founded on who Jesus is? If not, what might our good news look like if it was more closely coupled to its source?

What did 'salvation' mean to those who first encountered Jesus? How did they experience the Jesus revolution of healing, reconciliation and peace?

What might it mean for you to 'couple' your understanding of the gospel more closely to the actual words and works of Jesus? What would change? Would you welcome such a change?

● ● ●

ENCOUNTERING GOOD NEWS: ROGER ELLIS

Growing up, faith played little or no part in my upbringing. God was not on the agenda. My parents were Second World War survivors from a working class background and spent their lives pretty much living day by day apparently with little thought of the future.

BOUGHT A GUITAR TO PUNISH MY MA

An only child with plenty of attitude, I dropped out of education, disillusioned, living in the moment and living for the next experience. Rock music, festivals and the apparent counter culture was my only vision. In the words of Pink Floyd: 'You bought a guitar to punish your ma, you didn't like school and you know you're nobody's fool - Welcome to the Machine.' Around the age of 17-19 I began to question everything and realised what I saw as freedom was really just vacuous hedonism with a price tag at the end – emptiness! An amazing sequence of events saw me reading the Bible, having a powerful encounter with the Holy Spirit accompanied by an incredible conversion experience, being overwhelmed by God's love and his forgiveness, all accompanied by a life-possessing sense of calling and destiny.

PASSION FOR ALL THINGS JESUS

Undergirding all of this was my surprise at, fascination with, and passion for everything 'Jesus'. Ecclesiastical institution and religion had never been attractive. However as I read about the life of Jesus, I saw something completely different. Wine at weddings, the excluded welcomed, the underdog embraced, prostitutes forgiven, the oppressed released and the rich, self-righteous, powerful, upright and uptight given short shrift. Everything was equalised in Jesus, everybody was welcome, a new family was being built - his people. This was incredibly attractive but I was confused. If Jesus was God revealed to us, why is his good news apparently so at odds with religion? It seemed to me that God's agency on the earth, the church, was seriously 'missing the boat' somewhere. At this stage I just 'followed my passion' and the presence of God that it seemed I couldn't escape, not that I wanted to. It was wonderful! By the age of 23 I was leading a church, many people had found faith in Christ, and we were on fire for an experience of church with our friends which was all about love, sharing, relationships and the power of the

Spirit. We longed, and still long, for a community undergirded by God's word which changes the world (Acts 2:42-47). This journey, with its twists and turns, continues 30 years on![14]

LIVE IT TO GIVE IT

It seems to me that following Jesus is about faith in him; the power of his incarnation, life and teaching; the cross; the resurrection and our life in the Spirit that becomes the model for how we live life now. This is the good news that we receive and experience first so we can then 'live it and give it' away to others. It's good news for every individual that can transform every community. It's about both an inner rebirth and a social transformation. It's about God's rights, human rights, loving relationships, fathers and sons, men and women, people from every tribe, nation, people group and class. It's for rich, poor, men, women, old, young, gays, straights, the honest and dishonest, the whole and the broken, or however you see yourself or others see you. It breaks every barrier between humanity and God, every divide between human beings, and brings reconciliation to the heart of all creation. God is love and this good news is about love, humility, equality, joy and celebration. It's about peace and sustenance even in the midst of the suffering and pain that comes with being human and living on this planet. It's about Jesus who showed the way. It's about abundant life, the kingdom of Jesus, his wonderful reign and rule touching every part of creation, culture, life and humanity in anticipation of the day when 'heaven comes to earth' and God's love, justice and judgment become fully visible to all. Life is complicated. This world is fallen, and whenever human beings are involved, as well as wonderful things, there will be a big mess. The reason why some Christians are so constipated, miserable, judgmental, misogynistic, religious and up tight is that they were like that before they became Christians! The truth is that like all humanity, we, as followers of Jesus, desperately need the good news and to be continually transformed by the Holy Spirit. Without this we are destined to irrelevance.[15]

SUMMARY ///

The Gospel records point to good news because they point to Jesus. What does it mean to you to encounter Jesus as Good news today?

///

14   www.revelation.org.uk

15   See Roger Ellis, Essence: The Manifesto of Jesus, 2012

SOURCE CODE: JESUS
IN THE STORY OF GOD

The journey to the cross began long before. As the echo of the crunching of the fruit was still sounding in the garden, Jesus was leaving for Calvary.
Max Lucado[16]

An important aspect of rediscovering Jesus as the source of our gospel is the recognition that his coming has a setting, a place, in the wider story of God. Those who first encountered Jesus came to understand that he was more than a Messiah; that he was God himself, the creator, come to redeem his fallen world. They worshipped a Cosmic Christ, Jesus as the redeemer of all things. But they did so because of what they saw in Jesus and heard from him. The Jesus of the Gospels did not 'become' the Christ of salvation after his death and resurrection; salvation was embedded in his every word and action. The eye-witnesses of the life of Jesus saw him do things, heard him say things; experienced him in such a way that when they put the pieces of the puzzle together only one conclusion was

possible: God our maker, Yahweh the liberator of Israel has come to us in Jesus. And he has come to save us.

Tom Wright asserts that the stories collected for us in the Gospels - the miracles and interventions of Jesus - point in themselves to the wider truth of God's purposes in history:

'But suppose, just suppose, that the ancient prophetic dream had glimpsed a deeper truth. Suppose there were a god like Israel's God. Suppose this God did after all make the world. And suppose he were to claim, at long last, his sovereign rights over the world, not to destroy it (another philosophical mistake) or merely to 'intervene' in it from time to time ... but to fill it with his glory, to allow it to enter a new mode in which it would reflect his love, his generosity, his desire to make it over anew. Perhaps these stories are not, after all, the sort of bizarre things that people invent in retrospect to boost the image of a dead hero. ... Perhaps they are, instead, the sort of things that might just be characteristic of the new creation, of the fulfilled time, or what happens when heaven and earth come together.'[17]

'This is the unique, world-changing story at the heart of the gospel. The Christian message is good news precisely because it is about Jesus.
Name another religion where an omnipotent, omniscient and good God becomes human and dwells among us and dies for us. Name another religion that operates according to resurrection, and to grace.'[18]

16   www.aquotation.com/quote/max-lucado/journey-cross-began-long-before.html

17   N T Wright, Simply Jesus: A New Vision Of Who He Was, What He Did, And Why it Matters, London: Harper Collins, 2011

18   Carolyn Weber, Surprised by Oxford: A Memoir, Nashville: Thomas Nelson, 2011

HAIL TO THE KING!

For Wright and others it has become important to insist that Jesus does not come simply to 'save' people, but to declare God's kingship over the whole earth. Personal salvation - the possibility that an individual, though faith in Christ, can receive God's forgiveness and be reconciled to the Father - is a vital and very beautiful part of the story the Gospels tell. But it is not the whole story. This is not a new religious leader taking his place among history's holy men. This is the planet's king, claiming his throne and inviting his loyal subjects to join with him in a New Era of peace and joy. Jesus' life and death, and specifically his resurrection, inaugurate God's rule in a new way. To encounter Jesus Christ is not simply to meet a new guru, it is to come face to face with the world's maker and rightful monarch. To become a follower of Christ is to co-operate with him in bringing into present reality this new, peaceable kingdom. The Gospel story is the story of Jesus becoming king.

'It will not do to suppose that Jesus came to teach people "how to get to heaven". That view has been immensely popular in Western Christianity for many generations, but it simply won't do.' Wright insists, 'The whole point of Jesus's public career was not to tell people that God was in heaven and that, at death, they could leave "earth" behind and go to be with him there. It was to tell them that

God was now taking charge, right here on "earth"; that they should pray for this to happen; that they should recognise, in his own work, the signs that it was happening indeed; and that when he completed his work, it would become a reality.'[19]

For Tom Wright it is this idea of 'God becoming king' that most captures the message of the four Gospels: they are the story of how it is that God has come to us, and has at last become our king. It is to this claim that the miracles point, that the words direct us. It is to this claim that we are asked to respond. This is 'the devastating and challenging message I find in the four Gospels: God really has become king - in and through Jesus! A new state of affairs has been brought into existence. A door has been opened that nobody can shut. Jesus is now the world's rightful Lord, and all other lords must fall at his feet.'[20]

The 'kingdom of God', undisputed as a central idea on the teachings of Jesus, takes on new significance in this reading. If God is becoming king in Jesus then the kingdom is neither a place we can go to nor a future state we are waiting for. It is a person. 'The new proximity of the kingdom of which Jesus speaks - the distinguishing feature of his message,' Joseph Ratzinger writes, 'is to be found in Jesus himself. Through Jesus presence and action, God has here and now entered actively into history in a whole new way.... He himself is the treasure. Communion with him is the pearl of great price.'[21]

19   N T Wright, Simply Jesus: A New Vision Of Who He Was, What He Did, And Why it Matters, London: Harper Collins, 2011

20   Tom Wright, How God Became King: Getting to the Heart of the Gospels, London: SPCK, 2012

21   Pope Benedict XVI, Joseph Ratzinger, Jesus of Nazareth, New York: Doubleday, 2007

God
becoming
King

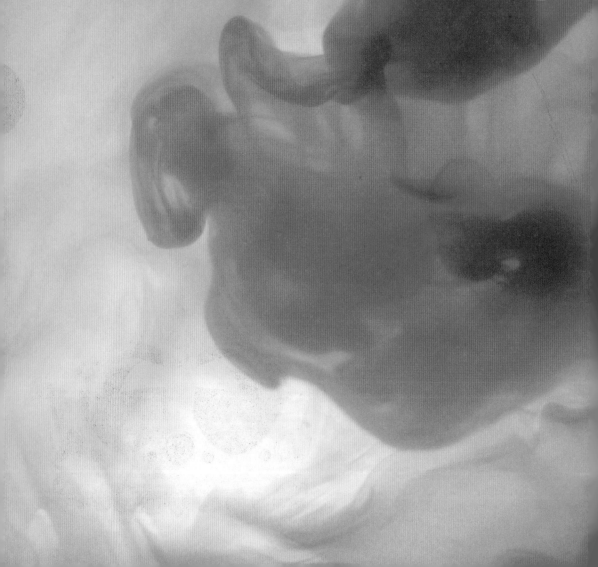

YOUR KINGDO[M]
YOUR WILL BE
ON EARTH AS

COME
DONE
IS IN HEAVEN

GOSPELING: A BIGGER, WIDER PICTURE?

'We need such a wider, deeper vision of the gospel, because all too often we interpret mission as entirely and exclusively to do with persuading other people to become Christians. Whether we call it evangelism, outreach or faith-sharing, it has the same goal: the numerical growth of the church, as individuals make the decision to convert. Recruitment becomes the overarching purpose of the church, and when we ask what we are recruiting people to do, the answer comes back 'to recruit others!' In this model the only growth that counts is numerical growth, and the sole focus of the kingdom is the conversion of the individual: not to a life of purpose and beauty, but to a life of converting others. At best this reduces the biblical vision of the kingdom to the narrow scope of individual salvation. At worst, it turns the whole enterprise into a pyramid selling scheme: an Amway model that our friends and neighbours are quite right to steer clear of.'[25]

But the mission of the church, Jurgen Moltmann reminds us, 'is not to spread the church but to spread the kingdom.'[26] There is a purpose for which we are 'saved', and this purpose has everything to do with God becoming king. This is the view of mission that is 'articulated in the New Testament and offered as the church's job description. In this view, God has established the church as the community in whom his intentions will be vested. He calls that community to work and pray for a very specific goal: the coming of his kingdom. This is further defined as the condition in which God's will is done on Earth. The mission of God is for the will of God to be done, and our participation in that process is our missional calling. Anything, in this view, that moves some aspect of the created order from rebellion to obedience, from God's will not being done to God's will being done, is missional.'[27]

Evangelism, mission, the announcing of the good news, revolves around this declaration that God has become our king in Jesus. This is the activity that Scot McKnight calls 'gospeling'. 'To gospel,' he says, 'is to announce the good news about key events in the life of Jesus Christ. To gospel for Paul was to tell, announce, declare, and shout aloud the story of Jesus Christ as the saving news of God.' But this is in the context of the whole story; the big picture of what it means that God is now king. 'Any real gospeling has to lay out the (whole) story of Scripture if it wants to put back the "good" into the good news.'[28]

How might it change your view of faith-sharing if you were to grasp this bigger, wider picture of Christ's coming? That the story you tell might not just be of sins forgiven – vital and important as that element may be - but of a world restored; of the brokenness that is both in us and around us fully and finally healed?

What if you could tell your neighbour that the God who made the world has not, contrary to popular rumour, abandoned it to its fate, but has launched a rescue plan and in that plan has provided for the healing of relationships and the ending of alienation in every sphere, from the personal to the cosmic: would that constitute good news?

25   Gerard Kelly, Church Actually: Rediscovering the Brilliance of God's Plan, Oxford: Lion Hudson, 2011

26   Jurgen Moltmann, cited in Veli-Matti Kärkkäinen, An Introduction to Ecclesiology: Ecumenical, Historical and Global Perspectives, IVP, 2002

27   Gerard Kelly, Church Actually: Rediscovering the Brilliance of God's Plan, Oxford: Lion Hudson, 2011

28   Scot McKnight, The King Jesus Gospel: The Original Good News Revisited, Grand Rapids: Zondervan, 2011

JESUS AND THE PEACEABLE KINGDOM[29]

The good news of Jesus is based on his message that the kingdom of God has come through him. Through his life, death and resurrection, Jesus brings God's reign into a fallen and hurting world and into the lives of people who desperately need his salvation. We often talk about the kingdom of God in terms of Jesus' manifesto of Luke 4, with its emphasis on proclaiming good news to the poor and setting the oppressed free. This is absolutely right, but is there also a broader dimension to Jesus' kingdom message that we might have missed? Richard Bauckham thinks that there is.

He makes the point that, although we tend to focus on Isaiah and Daniel, Jesus' kingdom theology would also have come very much from the Psalms, which he would have been brought up with. The Psalms feature the kingship and rule of God very prominently and these themes are closely related to the wider creation. The creation theology that we see in the Psalms tells us that God created all things; that he created them good, and that he is lovingly involved daily with their care. The non-human creation acknowledges that God rules now and looks forward to when he will reign in fullness, and they praise God and declare his glory.

Jesus would have had this broad (cosmic) understanding as a foundation to what he meant when he came proclaiming that the kingdom of God had come in him, as shown in the Lord's Prayer. Bauckham sees the phrase 'on earth as it is in heaven' as relating to each of the three petitions: ie, 'May your name be hallowed, may your kingdom come, and may your will be done, on earth as it is in heaven'. It can be easy to see the earth as simply a backdrop against which God's will is done in people's lives, but that is a misreading of what Jesus is teaching his disciples to pray!

Jesus' kingdom message thus encompasses the wider creation, as well as human beings. Two instances are particularly interesting in this regard.

The first is Jesus' temptation in the wilderness and Mark's description of Jesus as being 'with the wild animals' (Mark 1:13). In the Hebrew Bible, one of the things that was anticipated when God came to his people and reigned fully was that there would be peace throughout the created order: peace between wild and domestic animals, and peace between wild animals and humans. Isaiah 11:6-9 is the classic picture of this with its description of the wolf lying down with the lamb and the child putting its hand into the snake's nest.

When Jesus goes into the wilderness, Bauckham highlights that he meets three groups: Satan, the wild animals, and the angels. Satan is Jesus' enemy and the angels are his friends, but standing between them are the wild animals, enemies with whom Jesus makes friends. The phrase 'to be with someone' is used elsewhere by Mark to signify friendship (e.g. 3:14, 14:67) and is the phrase used of the animals in the ark (they were 'with' Noah). So here, Jesus makes peace between the human world and the wild animals in a way that begins to fulfil the Bible's future messianic hope.

The second instance is the stilling of the storm in Mark 4:35-41 (and its equivalents). This story reflects the ancient imagery of the primeval waters in the creation narrative, which God controlled by putting boundaries around it and giving it limits, hence creating a stable environment for life. But these waters were only confined not fully abolished. When Jesus speaks to the wind and the sea he evokes the way that God spoke to the waters of chaos at the dawn of creation. 'What Jesus enacts, therefore, is the Creator's pacification of chaos. In this small-scale instance he anticipates the final elimination of all forces of destruction that will distinguish the renewed creation from the present.'[30]

Jesus is the Lord of all creation, the one through whom and for whom all things have been created (Colossians 1:16). When we read the Gospels with that belief in our minds, we might find we discover some surprising new things!

---

29   Ruth Valerio, based on Richard Bauckham, 'Reading the Synoptic Gospels Ecologically' in Living With Other Creatures: Green Exegesis and Theology, Paternoster Press, 2012

30 Ruth Valerio, based on Richard Bauckham, 'Reading the Synoptic Gospels Ecologically' in Living With Other Creatures: Green Exegesis and Theology, Paternoster Press, 2012

PRE-ORDER NOW
AVAILABLE JULY 2013

Spring Harvest

LIVE WORSHIP FROM SPRING HARVEST 2013

Spirit-soaked live worship from
Spring Harvest's Big Top

LEAD WORSHIPPERS

MARK BESWICK   PETE JAMES   LARA MARTIN   CHRIS McCLARNEY   NOEL ROBINSON

Available from EssentialChristian.com
or your local Christian bookstore

essential christian

Seed
of
hope

CREATION REGAINED?

Hans Kung describes this as 'The essential difference and superiority of the Christian message, when compared to other oriental religions of redemption.' The aim of the Christian faith, he suggests, 'is not the salvation of the individual alone and the freeing of the individual soul from suffering, sin and death. The essential part of the Christian message is the idea of salvation for the whole community of people, of which the individual is a member.'[31]

'Along the road of salvation, I may discover the inestimable joy of being included. I may rejoice to name myself as 'saved'. But this does not begin to capture the depth and the breadth of God's plan. To take my place in God's plan is to become a part of something bigger and richer and deeper and wider than I can even hope to understand.'[32]

This message is good news to our world because it carries a seed of hope; a dream of a world made new. In the timeless phrase of Al Wolters, the message of the gospel is Creation Regained.[33] Rooted in the events of the Gospels themselves, and not least in the resurrection of Jesus, this seed of hope speaks to every dark circumstance we might face, even today. 'The Easter stories come at the end of the four Gospels.' Tom Wright explains, 'But they are not about an "end". They are about a beginning. The beginning of God's new world. The beginning of the kingdom. ...God will do for the whole cosmos, in the end, what he did for Jesus at Easter; the risen Jesus is, remember, the prototype of the new creation. God will do this through Jesus himself; the ascended Jesus, remember, is the ruler within the new creation as it bursts in upon the old. And God will do it through the presence of the risen and ascended Jesus when he comes to heal, to save and also to judge.'[34]

The message of the kingdom and the message of the cross are one and the same. It is through the cross that God becomes king. It is through the death and resurrection of Jesus that the re-making of the world becomes possible. Kingdom theology is not a retreat from the cross, but an embracing of it. The gospel truly is, as it turns out, the heart of the Gospels. Last word on this important subject from Tom Wright:

'We have, alas, belittled the cross, imagining it merely as a mechanism for getting us off the hook of our own petty naughtiness or as an example of some general benevolent truth. It is much, much more. It is the moment when the story of Israel reaches its climax; the moment when, at last, the watchmen on Jerusalem's walls see their God coming in his kingdom; the moment when the people of God are renewed so as to be, at last, the royal priesthood who will take over the world not with the love of power but with the power of love; the moment when the kingdom of God overcomes the kingdoms of the world. It is the moment when a great old door, locked and barred since our first disobedience, swings open suddenly to reveal not just the garden, opened once more to our delight, but the coming city, the garden city that God has always planned and is now inviting us to go through the door and build with him. The dark power that stood in the way of this kingdom-vision has been defeated, overthrown, rendered null and void. Its legions will still make a lot of noise and cause a lot of grief, but the ultimate victory is now assured. This is the vision the evangelists offer us as they bring together the kingdom and the cross.'[35]

31   Hans Kung, The Church, Continuum, 2001, p272, cited in Veli-Matti Kärkkäinen, An Introduction to Ecclesiology: Ecumenical, Historical and Global Perspectives, IVP, 2002

32   Gerard Kelly, Church Actually: Rediscovering the Brilliance of God's Plan, Oxford: Lion Hudson, 2011

33   Al Wolters, Creation Regained: Biblical Basics for a Reformational Worldview, Eerdmans, 1985 and 2005

34   N T Wright, Simply Jesus: A New Vision Of Who He Was, What He Did, And Why it Matters, London: Harper Collins, 2011

35   Tom Wright, How God Became King: Getting To The Heart of the Gospels, London: SPCK, 2012

Words and Works. How do you see 'the words and works' of Jesus, in the light of this announcement that 'God has become King?' Does a kingdom reading of the Gospels alter your perspective? If so, how?

How might a 'bigger, wider picture' of the work of Christ change the way you follow him? What new avenues might it open up for you in mission and worship? How might the message of 'Creation Regained' be received by your friends and neighbours?

Is there a model of salvation you can work from that includes the personal, offering hope for freedom from sin, but touches, also, on the wider scope of the kingdom?

KEEPING THE CROSS AT THE CENTRE

It remains vital to recognise, in the wider view of the kingdom gospel we are proposing, that the events of Easter remain at the very centre of our faith. A wider kingdom vision does not reduce the cross - anything but. Rather, it sees the cross - the death and resurrection of Jesus - as the climactic point at which God's new kingship is paid for and delivered. Whatever God intends to do to renew the created order, it is because of the cross, and by the cross, that he will do it. This same principle applies to personal salvation. The assertion here is that the work of Christ is bigger than personal salvation, but not smaller. It includes the vital, life-changing dimension of personal salvation. To move to a wider view of God's kingdom project is not to leave behind the 'old old story' of salvation: it is to set it in its rightful context as part of the mind-boggling, game-changing wonder of God's plan.

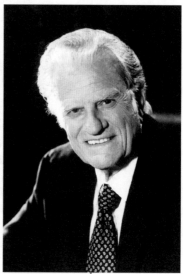

KNOWING JESUS – SIMPLY

In a moving and remarkable book called Simply Jesus, Joseph M Stowell tells the story of two high-profile Christian leaders of the twentieth century:

The meal was just about to finish when I leaned over and asked Billy Graham the question I had hoped to ask him all evening. Martie and I had been seated next to Dr Billy Graham at a dinner for the staff and board of his organisation. Billy, 80 at the time, was lucid and interesting. Wondering what he would say about the highest joys in life, I asked, 'of all of your experiences in ministry, what have you enjoyed the most?' Then (thinking I might help him out a little) I quickly added, was it your time spent with presidents and heads of state? Or was it...' Before I could finish my next sentence, Billy swept his hand across the table cloth, as if to push my suggestions onto the floor.

'None of that', he said 'By far the greatest joy of my life has been fellowship with Jesus. Hearing him speak to me, having him guide me, sensing his presence with me and his power through me. This has been the highest pleasure of my life!'

It was spontaneous, unscripted and clearly unrehearsed. There wasn't even a pause. With a life of stellar experiences and worldwide fame behind him, it was simply Jesus who was on his mind and on his heart. His lifelong experience with Jesus had made its mark, and Billy was satisfied.

I found Billy Graham's statement that evening more than convicting. I found it motivating right to the core of my being. With everything in me, I want what he's experienced. I find my heart saying, 'If I make it to 80, I want to say the same thing.' Even more so when you consider the story of Chuck Templeton.

Templeton's name was practically a household word in evangelical homes in the fifties and sixties. He pastored one of Toronto's leading churches and – along with his close friend Billy Graham – helped found Youth for Christ Canada. His extraordinary ability to communicate God's word put him in demand on platforms across North America. But I don't remember him for his stellar gifts. I remember him for his renunciation of the faith.

Evangelicals everywhere were rocked by the news that Chuck Templeton had left his church and renounced all he had previously embraced and proclaimed. The former preacher went on to fame and fortune. He managed two of Canada's leading newspapers, worked his way into an influential position with the Canadian Broadcasting Company - and even took a run at the prime minister's office. It had been decades since I'd thought of Chuck Templeton. So imagine my surprise when I noticed he had been interviewed by Lee Strobel in his book A Case for Faith. After reading Templeton's most recent book Farewell to God: My Reason for Rejecting the Christian Faith, Strobel caught a plane to Toronto to meet with him. Though 83 and in declining health, the former preacher vigorously defended his agnostic rejection of a God who claimed to be love, yet allowed suffering across the world to go unchecked.

Then, towards the end of their time together, Strobel asked Templeton point-blank how he felt about Jesus. Instantly, the old man softened. He spoke in adoring terms about Jesus, concluding, 'In my view he is the most important human being who has ever existed.' Then, as his voice began to crack, he haltingly said 'I...miss...him.' With that, Strobel writes, tears flooded Templeton's eyes and his shoulders bobbed as he wept.

Think of it, Billy Graham and Chuck Templeton, two friends who chose radically different paths through life. And near the end of their journeys, one has found Jesus to be his prized possession, while the other weeps for having left him long ago.[36]

---

36 Joseph M Stowell, Simply Jesus, Oregon, Multnomah Press, 2002

REFLECTION

Reflecting on Stowell's moving account, Patrick Regan writes of his own commitment to finding Jesus at the centre of a challenging and complex ministry:

For me I have always been a bit scared that I will end up like Chuck Templeton. I know that's not what a Christian leader should be saying: the reality is when you have to deal with a mother whose 16-year-old son has been stabbed though the heart and as a result killed, kids who have been abused by adults, children who you know will die of a preventable disease soon after you leave them - it really affects you. It can make you feel helpless as you so want to make life better for them, but you can't. I know the theological answers to some of the big questions to do with suffering; I have even preached on them, but still it doesn't make it any easier. Then you step into the Christian culture and you see us arguing about things which seem so small; saying we love each other, but in reality gossiping behind each other's back. I find the quest for power confusing, and the latest new announcement of the new thing God is doing.

Life is complex and we are so fragile, when I strip everything back, my past experiences, my frustrations, my fears of being misunderstood, I try and look again at the person of Jesus. I find myself finding hope again that Jesus moved into our neighbourhood and decided to go through all this stuff with us. It doesn't mean all the questions go away, yet you realise the kingdom Jesus came to bring is so much bigger than what we have made it and Christ is so much more passionate than I am about restoring it. I find myself not wanting to abandon ship but wanting to be part of the journey. In the process of that journey I am learning slowly to let Christ speak to me about his world and his love for me and in doing so, I pray I will stay close and at the end of my life I will not have to say I MISS HIM.[37]

SUMMARY

The good news announced in the Gospels is more than personal salvation: it is that God has come to establish his kingdom on Earth. Everything changes at the cross. What does it mean to you to embrace and proclaim this kingdom today?

● ● ●

INTERLUDE: JOHN ON
PATMOS

Niall Williams is an Irish-American novelist much-loved for his explorations of the joys and complexities of human love. In John[38] he explores a different kind of love altogether. Sitting in his garden one day, taking a break from work on another project, he was struck, he says, by a single question. 'The question came to me out of the blue,' he says, 'It was: What was John doing the day before he wrote the Gospel?' The question resulted in a year of research, reading John's Gospel, but also extensive works of history and commentary around it, and around John himself. The result is a novel 'depicting the inner life of a man of faith and doubt, and, most important, perhaps, what it might be to love for a lifetime'.

This extract tells of the moment, old and nearing death, when John, the last of the Apostles, discovers the true purpose of his life:

The storm crashes yet, the dark more dark still, all the world bowed and blinded. And now here, in John, is again revelation. Here is vision of time itself, of all things temporal and not. He knows. He knows as he has not before what is finite and what infinite. He knows that for light, darkness is needed and that his 100 years is not an end but a beginning only. He raises up his hands, and it is as though to word sent long ago, response is now received. His voice cries out a prayer.

38   Niall Williams, John, Bloomsbury Publishing, 2009

And here in the illumined room of his spirit he sees a church, a vast lit place to which keep coming men, women and children, innumerable as stars. The church fills and further fills, its walls expanding; his spirit rises like an eagle and sees the throng stretch into the greater distance, yea onto the horizon of sea and sky itself.

'Hall'luyah, Hall'luyah,' he cries and the disciples look to one another in awe and joy of what immanence is made manifest. Here is rapture and revelation. 'Hall'luyah, Hall'luyah!' Here is an ecstasy of soul, a condition out of ancient Scripture, a purity of communion not known nor considered actual in their old age of the world. But here it is. Here is man with God. Here are all things made new.

John sees.

Returned to him is every moment from the first to the last and beyond. Returned to him in perfect clarity is each instant he spent by the side of Jesus. Each word spoken is in his mind. The teachings are as scribed on fresh papyrus. All is recollected. In those moments while the storm beats and flashes, he himself is the book being written.

Here are things he had forgotten. Not the details of sunlight nor the scent of the olive trees, not the salt slap of the Sea of Tiberias nor the close heat of Cana, but words, ways of saying. Everything taught, each phrase Jesus said is here now. And in that moment John knows the testament is not himself but the Word, and that what remains and what will remain to the last is just this, the Word he carries.

What gift he bears is not a narrative, is not a telling of what happened, but something other; it is a vision for all time, it is the very cornerstone of the vast church that looms in his mind.

He sees.

He sees and is humbled and uplifted both. He sees as if from a great height and is consoled.

The storm raging still, he lowers his arms. He speaks the names of the disciples gathered there, and tells them not to fear.

He says, 'The lord is with us.' Then he asks that one of them will write what he will tell.

He sits. A light is lit.
In voice clear and strong, he begins to tell of the Baptist: 'There was a man sent from God whose name was John...'

///

The author described John remembering 'in perfect clarity ... each instant he spent by the side of Jesus' and suggests that this remembering is 'the very cornerstone of the vast church that looms in his mind'. This is a fictionalised picture of the apostle pouring all that he remembers of Jesus into his Gospel narrative. Does this imaginative picture help you to grasp just how the Gospels that we have today came into being? How might this process help you to find 'The gospel in the Gospels?'

Formule à 14,50 €

ENTRÉE + PLAT OU PLAT + DESSERT
Starter + MAIN COURSE or MAIN course + Dessert

Carpaccio de saumon vinaigrette à l'aneth
Thinly sliced raw salmon with a dill dressing

Mesclun de salade façon Ambassade "
mixed green salade

Velouté crémeux de légumes
Crème of végétable soup

Penne aux quatre fromages
Pasta with a four cheese sauce

Boeuf carotte ou PLAT DU JOUR (1er)
Beef casserole with carrots or MAIN COURSE OF DAY (1er)

Filet de saumon rôti pommes écrasées
Roast salmon fillet with mashed potatoes

Tarte aux pommes glace vanille
Apple tart with vanilla ice cream

Salade de fruits frais
Fresh fruit salad

Nougat glacé, coulis de fruits rouges
Nougat ice cream with red berries

menu à 29,50 €

Carpaccio de boeuf copeaux de parmesan
Thinly sliced raw beef with slivers of Parmesan cheese

Douzaine d'escargots de Bourgogne
A dozen snails in garlic butter

Oeuf cocotte toasts au Jambon Serrano
coddled egg with cured spanish ham and toast

Ravioli à la ricotta epinards sauce tomate
Ravioli with ricotta cheese and spinach in a tomato sauce

Entrecôte grillée pommes Pont neuf sauce béarnaise
Grilled entrecôte steak with fried potatoes

Escalope de veau poêlée pâtes fraîches sauce champignon
Pan fried veal escalope with fresh pasta in a mushroom sauce

Cuisse de canard confit pommes sarladaises
confit of duck leg with thinly sliced potatoes baked butter

Duo de poisson sauce citron
Too fish fillets with a lemon sauce

ou Plat du JOUR (2e)
or main course of day (2e)

Plateau de fromage
Cheese

Tiramisu
Italian coffee flavoured dessert with mascapone cheese

Moelleux au chocolat
Rich chocolate pudding with custard sauce

Crème brûlée à l'orange
orange crème brûlée

ENDWORD: BE, SAY, DO

It is through all that we have seen here that we are able to proclaim that Jesus is 'good news'. He is good news to those he encounters in his earthly ministry, saying and doing things that bring breakthrough, healing and joy to all around. But he is good news in a deeper sense still. Through his death and resurrection he brings the ultimate Exodus, the freeing of the creation itself from its slavery to death. The good news that Jesus brings is cosmic in scope. It is fully expressed in the particular and specific acts of his ministry – the healing of a man born blind, the transformation of a Samaritan woman, the feeding of 5,000 hungry people - but it is so much more. His particular acts point us to his broader purpose, and his death and resurrection make both - the micro and the macro - possible.

Most people who have never actually read the menu probably assume they can order à la carte at the Jesus table or customise their own recipe of faith.

'But you can't say yes to the historical figure and a few parables but pass on miracles, the resurrection, and the Son-of-God thing. That is not the offering. Christ is a fixed meal. It is all or nothing with his claims. Everyone is invited, but only you can decide if you actually want to eat at his table. For those who do believe in Christ, it means getting real, being honest about your sin, and living your life as if you really mean it.'[39]

So what does this mean for us, 2,000 years after the events described in the Gospels? Is it possible that the significance of these events can still reach and change us? If so, it will do so in the same dimensions we have seen in the life of Christ.

It will impact our identity, our words and our actions. If Jesus came not only to make possible the rescue of individuals, but also to proclaim God's coming rule over all the earth, then our encounter with him will radically change:

- **Who we are.** We are hearers of the good news of God, recipients of his grace and mercy, the object of his limitless love. We are his beloved.

- **What we say.** We have a word of hope to speak not only to individuals but to whole cultures - even to the creation itself. The bondage of our brokenness is ended. Freedom has come. Our story need not end in death. We can speak life.

- **What we do.** The kingdom Jesus has announced is not a world of words alone. It is embodied in action, demonstrated in love lived out. There is a 'now' of the kingdom to experience as well as a 'not yet' to proclaim. We don't just talk about God's rule, we live it.

Through receiving the good news of Christ we will become good news, in who we are, in what we say and in what we do. The question we must face today is whether we have truly embraced what it means to Be, Say and Do good news in our culture. 'That is the bizarre thing about the good news: who knows how you will really hear it one day, but once you have heard it, I mean really heard it, you can never unhear it. Once you have read it, or spoken it, or thought it, even if it irritates you, even if you hate hearing it or cannot find it feasible, or try to dismiss it, you cannot unread it, or unspeak it, or unthink it.'[40]

---

39   Carolyn Weber, Surprised by Oxford: A Memoir, Nashville: Thomas Nelson, 2011

40   Carolyn Weber, Surprised by Oxford: A Memoir, Nashville: Thomas Nelson, 2011

ENCOUNTERING GOOD NEWS: ALAN CHARTER

What does it mean for me to Be, Say and Do good news?

BE

So, to start with the hardest - being good news. The challenge here is that it is really about who I am and how I live and that can be a bit scary ...especially because I know 'me' and I know the times that I'm not being good news! That said, it is actually more about the way that I live in light of God's grace and thankfully that truly is amazing and boundless! Working with children and young people and those who work with them, as well as being a parent, brings it all into focus. The old adage that children learn what they live has a lot going for it. I want my life to reveal God's grace and goodness as much as I can. I know that I am a product of God's grace and I long for any child or young person that I encounter to know God's love and grace for themselves. I hope I live it, so that they can experience it in some small way!

SAY DO

One of the ways that I get to speak out the good news is in a couple of local schools that I've invested time in. I've been going into one of these schools for 15 years and it has been great to speak to the children regularly about what the good news means to me as well as getting to know God through the pages of the Bible. Seeing the children grow with each year group working their way through the school is quite special – particularly when I get to give each of them a little gift of a book called 'It's your move' to help them as they prepare for the big transition into secondary school. It is a great moment when they recount some of the stories or anecdotes that have been shared over the years and relate them to their own stories.

As a family, in a small way we've been living out a new chapter of what it means to 'Do good news' over the last three years, since welcoming our youngest daughter by adoption in 2009. There is a huge need to provide homes for the thousands of children in the UK care system ...and as the story of the starfish goes, we can't impact them all but we can make a difference for this one! The reality is that in spite of the hard work that it can involve on occasions, we've been blown away by the goodness of God through the whole experience. The family adventure continues as we work with our local authority on the next step to help give a temporary home to children through fostering. We're not expecting it to be plain sailing, but we do know that God's love and grace have been sufficient for all we've needed so far and have no doubt of that changing anytime soon.[41]

---

41   Alan Charter is Head of Evangelism for Scripture Union, www.scriptureunion.org.uk, and Director of Children Matter! He is an Advisor to the Spring Harvest Theme Group.

HUMANS ARE THE VITAL INGREDIENT IN GOD'S KINGDOM PROJECT. WHEN WE ASK ABOUT THE WAY IN WHICH GOD WANTS TO RUN THE WORLD AND THEN FOCUS THIS ON THE SHARPER QUESTION OF HOW JESUS NOW RUNS THE WORLD, WE SHOULD EXPECT, FROM THE WHOLE OF SCRIPTURE, THAT THE ANSWER WILL HAVE SOMETHING TO DO WITH THE DELEGATION OF GOD'S AUTHORITY, OF JESUS'S AUTHORITY, TO HUMAN BEINGS.... JESUS RESCUED HUMAN BEINGS IN ORDER THAT THROUGH THEM HE MAY RULE HIS WORLD IN THE NEW WAY HE ALWAYS INTENDED.

N T Wright

BE

[TWO]

INTRO: COLOSSIANS 1:6-9

'Living a life like Jesus must begin with being a student of Jesus. This is the seed of discipleship.'[42]

Carl Medearis

Paul addresses his friends in the church at Colosse in celebration of the work the good news is achieving. To do so, he speaks twice about fruit. In verse 6 he celebrates the fruit of changed lives, and includes his readers in this crop. In this sense they are the fruit of the good news. But later, in verse 9, he tells them he is praying for them, that they will go on to bear good fruit as they grow in God. In this second sense they produce the fruit of the good news. Fruit, then is what we are and what we produce. The good news addresses our identity before it addresses productivity. God does not ask us to make anything until he has asked us to be something. At this stage in our exploration of Jesus as the source of good news, we want to ask what it means for us, as his followers, to BE good news in all the places we are called to.

WHAT ARE THE KEY GOALS FOR THIS STAGE OF OUR JOURNEY?

1. The first is motivation - we want to paint a picture of what it means to find our identity in Christ so that we will want nothing more than to pursue the encounter that can make this real.

2. The second is resource - we want to identify and explore practical and useful tools and ideas to guide God's people in finding their identity in Christ and being his good news in their world.

We also hope, in the course of this journey, to find space and time within our event to make a fresh encounter with Jesus possible.

If we are truly to follow Jesus, to be good news people, we will have to come to terms with this dual emphasis. Before anything else, God speaks to who we are. The good news is good news for us. It is only out of this redeemed identity, out of who we are in Christ, that we can hope to bear fruit in the world. And once we know who we are, God speaks of where we are. Our location, the place and time we find ourselves in. Like Jesus, we are born into a specific tribe and neighbourhood; to particular people, at a certain time in history. The people of Colosse were not called to bear fruit in Coventry. The good news bears fruit in who we are. And through our lives, the good news bears fruit where we are. This means that our choice to live as followers of Christ calls us to be present to God and at the same time to be present to our world: to find the Holy Spirit at work in the who of our identity and in the where of our location.

42   Carl Medearis, Speaking Of Jesus: The Art Of Not-Evangelism, Colorado Springs, David C Cook, 2011

ACCEPTING GOD'S ACCEPTANCE

'He was the merciless taskmaster always standing over me yelling, "NOT ENOUGH I want MORE" He was always there, waving damnation in my face, saying, "If you want my approval, there's something else you must do." His constant demands were driving me insane. The more I strived to walk in his ways, the less love I felt for him. The more closely my feet followed him, the more my heart ran away.'[44]

These words, from American author J D Greear, reflect the experience of too many of Christ's followers the world over. Having encountered the good news of Jesus, we all too soon become victims of the bad news of religion, trapped by our own incapacity to please God. Rowan Williams writes: 'The God of the Bible, and above all the God of Jesus, is not our rival or our examiner or our prosecutor but our lover. There is nothing we can do to impress him or put him in our debt. If we start from the assumption that we have to do these things, we shall become either deludedly arrogant or despairing. If we allow ourselves to be lured out of these fictions and prisons, we see that our utter inability to acquire a satisfactory and impressive spiritual life is the best possible news, because then we can simply put ourselves in his hands, trusting in his love.'[45]

It is in this sense that following Jesus is not a religious experience at all. 'Religion,' Timothy Keller writes, 'as the default mode of our thinking and practices, is based upon performance: "I obey; therefore I am accepted by God." The basic operating principle of the gospel, however, is, not-surprisingly, an about-face, one of unmerited acceptance: "I am accepted by God through Christ; therefore I obey."'[46]

WHO WE ARE: BEING
PRESENT TO GOD

'The organ for seeing God is the heart. The intellect alone is not enough.'
Joseph Ratzinger [43]

One of the reasons many followers of Christ find it hard to share the good news of the gospel with others is that they themselves have not experienced it as good news. They want to offer others grace, but they themselves are tied-up in religion. They want to announce forgiveness, but they themselves feel condemned. They want to proclaim mercy, but judge themselves all too severely. The only answer is to let the coming of Jesus be good news for us before it is good news through us. We have to receive before we can share; to be freed before we try to free others. What does the good news say to us and about us before it asks us to say anything to others?

43   Joseph Ratzinger, Pope Benedict XVI, translated from the German by Adrian J Walker, Jesus of Nazareth, Doubleday, 2007

44   J D Greear, Gospel: Recovering the Power that Made Christianity Revolutionary, Nashville: B and H, 2011

45   Rowan Williams in the foreword to Ruth Burrows OCD, Love Unknown: The Archbishop of Canterbury's Lent Book 2012, London: Continuum, 2011

46   Tim Keller in the foreword to J D Greear, Gospel: Recovering the Power that Made Christianity Revolutionary, Nashville: B and H, 2011

Perhaps we need to rediscover the way the Bible talks about 'religion' – as obedient discipleship because of God's grace. So James can urge his readers to pursue true religion (James 1:27) as doers of the word of God once they have believed: to be properly religious is to be seized by the grace and love of God and to live in that love.

This is the heart of the message Jesus came to share with us, that the heart of God is both filled and fuelled by love. 'In human beings,' Brennan Manning says, 'Love is a quality, a highly-prized virtue; in God, love is his identity. ... For his love

in never, never, never based on our performance, never conditioned by our moods - of elation or depression. The furious love of God knows no shadow of alteration or change. It is reliable. And always tender.'[47]

The only answer is to let the gospel impact us before we ask what its impact on others might be. We must receive before we expect to share.

This means that our encounter with Jesus will not just change our religious affiliation, but will speak into us an entirely new identity. We are who God says we are, not who we imagine ourselves to be.

47   Brennan Manning, The Furious Longing of God, Colorado Springs: David C Cook, 2009

● ● ●

ENCOUNTERING GOOD NEWS: VIRGINIA LUCKETT

I have come to glimpse that as Christians, we believe in a God so big there are no words we can use to fully describe him. Time means nothing to God. He is alpha and omega, he is not trapped by space or dimensions – he is omnipresent, all mighty, able to be in all times, all space, all past, all present and all possible futures, all at the same time... so powerful, just his words from his mouth created life. Awesome, awe inspiring, awe-full. This is our God.

And all that divinity was concentrated down and walked the earth 2,000 years ago as Jesus Christ. In John 15:12-17 we hear this Jesus say 'You did not choose me, but I chose you.' St Paul tells us in Ephesians 1:4,

> 'For he chose us in him before the creation of the world to be holy and blameless in his sight.'

WOW! The God who made the universe chose me for holiness before the creation of the world.... What a profound, life changing truth.

Each of us was chosen, was born in the heart of God before the creation of the world. When the earth was a formless void and darkness covered the face of the deep (Genesis 1:3) God already had us in his sights. I am not a mistake, I am not the product of chance or the random collision of atoms, I was chosen.

When I try to wrestle with this truth, my emotions are often conflicted - why would God do that? Why me? But I have come to glimpse that it's because God is love (1 John 4:8). Without God there would be no love. We can only love as humans because God is love; it's through our Christlikeness, or being made in the image of God, that we have any capacity to be able to love others, because God is the source, the creator, the instigator of all love. And what has been good news for me is that this Jesus Christ, our God, is always calling us into relationship with him; he relentlessly chooses us, he wants to call us his friends. He wants us to be as close to him as if we were like a branch on a large plant, a vine - fed, nourished, growing, supported and fruitful. He loves us with passion so strong he was prepared to die for us. He desires us. It's an awe inspiring thing to be loved by God!

But as we all know, from our own human relationships, we can't force someone to love us, loving is a two way thing, both parties have to choose. No amount of Jesus relentlessly choosing us, calling us, loving us, is any good unless we respond.

Question is: will you let him love you? Will you give him your deepest places, your whole self and just let him... love you? I pray this Spring Harvest we will all experience the passionate love of Christ.[48]

---

48   Virginia Luckett is Head of UK Church Relationships at Tearfund, www.tearfund.org

A NEW IDENTITY?

Brian Draper contrasts this identity, founded on the person of Christ, with the shallow and hollow dreams of a consumerist culture: 'Our ultimate source of identity,' he writes, 'does not spring from our dominant capitalist worldview, which tells us that we need to purchase and consume in order to become who we truly are. Somewhere deep down, something whispers the real alternative: that it is in our nakedness, our stripped-bare self, that we are most fully open to the possibilities of becoming the person we were born to be.'[49]

Using even more dramatic language, Scotsman Timothy Neat says: 'It may be that, in the long term, the growth, vigour and beauty of Western materialism will prove to have been not the life-giving dynamism of youth but a malignant cancer in the throat of the world'[50]

Is it possible, in the midst of the many voices telling us who we are, or what we need to be truly fulfilled, to hear the voice of Jesus clearly? What do you need to do for that one, most important voice, to become clearer?

The intense relevance of this to our present culture should not be missed. The search for identity - the need to be named and known - is central to our humanity. Alison Morgan comments on the impact of this on young people:

'A 2006 survey for National Kids Day found that children under ten identified celebrity as their top priority;[51] an NUT survey of teachers in 2008 found that two thirds said their pupils aspire to be sports stars or pop singers; many seek to be famous with no discernible talent. As the NUT remarks, 'this compounds the subsequent sense of failure, alienation and low self-esteem when celebrity status is not achieved.'[52]

What might it take for you to centre your life on this new identity; to shape your thoughts and actions on the reality that you are who God says you are? How might your understanding and practice of the gospel change?

49   Brian Draper, Spiritual Intelligence: A New Way of Being, Oxford: Lion Hudson, 2009

50   Timothy Neat, When I was young: Voices from Lost Communities in Scotland, cited in Alison Morgan, The Word on the Wind: Renewing Confidence in the Gospel, Oxford: Monarch Books, 2011

51   Andrew Johnson and Andy McSmith, The Independent, 18 December 2006

52   Nicola Woodcock, The Times, 14 March 2008, cited in Alison Morgan, The Word on the Wind: Renewing Confidence in the Gospel, Oxford: Monarch Books, 2011

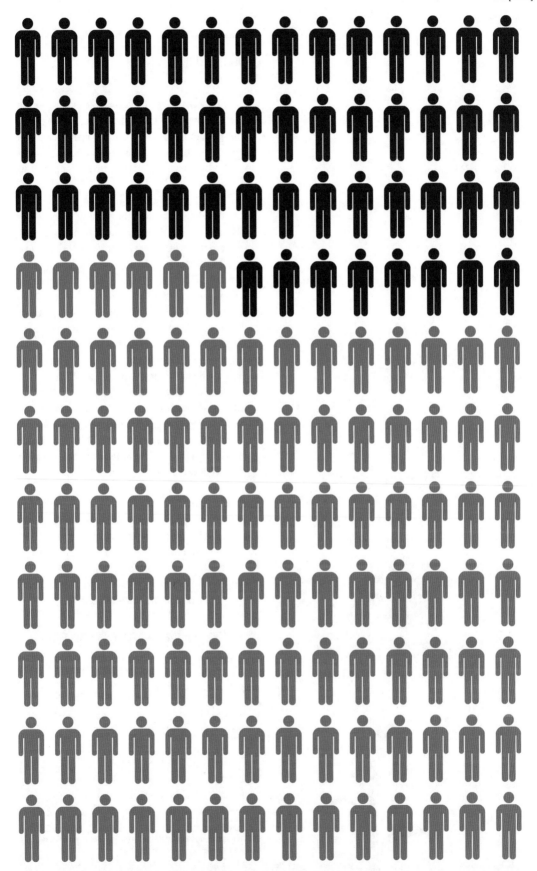

CHANGE YOUR RHYTHM

Part of the challenge of coming to a new sense of identity lies with taking the time to hear God, creating rhythms in which God's voice to us is not drowned out by every other voice. Paula Gooder describes her own experience of recognising this vital reality:

'As with so many things, the quality of our lives is shaped not so much by what we do but by how we do it. It is so easy to trudge through life, simply missing the gems and wonder of everyday existence, not because they are absent but because we don't notice them. I remember an occasion when my daughters were small, when one of them squealed in ecstasy, saying, 'Look, Mummy, look.' I looked and what I saw was a somewhat grubby patch of grass - with rather more mud than makes a parent, who has to do the washing, happy - which was dotted with a few, to my eye, miserable looking daisies. She hopped out of the pushchair and rushed over to them, and crouched down as low as she could get. 'Look,' she said, 'They've got pink edges right on the end, and the petals are like a fan and the yellow bit is all furry.'

She was right, of course, as anyone who has examined a daisy up close will tell you. What she was even more right about was that the somewhat ordinary muddy patch of grass held a treasure which I had completely overlooked. This is expressed much better than I could ever do by Saunders Lewis in his poem 'A Daisy in April'.

'Yesterday I saw a daisy
Like a shining mirror of the dawn.
The day before I walked over it without thought.
Yesterday I saw.'[53]

---

53   Paula Gooder, Everyday God: The Spirit of the Ordinary, Norwich: Canterbury Press, 2012

The late Henri Nouwen always taught that 'I am only free to love others when I can know myself as the beloved.'[54] Prayer is not simply the mechanism of supply-and-demand by which God gets his work done on the earth: it is the language by which he reaches us, transforming our hearts, breaking us open until our lives sing with new joy.

Before you think of 'doing things' for God, will you take the time to let God show you - deeply and fully and to the point where you are utterly convinced - what it is that he has done for you?

NEW RESOURCES FOR AN ANCIENT JOURNEY

Two books on prayer, both recently published, offer new insights into the ways in which being 'present to God' can work out in our post-modern, complex world.

Mystically Wired: Exploring New Realms in Prayer[55] is the work of Vineyard Pastor Ken Wilson. Wilson has for many years combined a personal commitment to prayer with a passionate interest in science, not least the science of the brain. This book brings the two together, suggesting that prayer is an essential and necessary human activity. He finds great encouragement in ancient practices, and offers practical suggestions for the development of a deeply satisfying life of prayer for today. Wilson's work is unusual and will particularly appeal to those wanting to deepen their experience of prayer and who are drawn to the meditative or contemplative approach. He writes at the intersection of contemporary / charismatic spirituality and more traditional / liturgical approaches, and offers some genuine ways forward.

Cave Refectory Road: monastic rhythms for contemporary living[56] is a UK publication from Anglican priest Ian Adams. Well-known to many

exploring alternative expressions of church and worship, Adams is convinced that in the models and practices of ancient monastic spirituality there are resources that are both relevant and applicable to postmodern settings. He bases his explorations on the three 'contexts' of monastic life – the cave in which the seeker of God is alone, the refectory in which community is expressed, and the road on which holy wanderings reveal more of who God is. From each of these contexts Adams draws out practical resources for contemporary prayer.

One overwhelming similarity between these two books is the assertion that to be effective, prayer must involve significant time and focus. Both authors provide insight into this reality, and suggestions as to how it can be achieved - but neither suggests that 'being present to God' can be experienced without intentional rhythms and focussed time. As in any relationship, communion with God requires communication, and the lesson of the ancients is, in this, startlingly relevant for today.

JUDGE NOT...

The impact of finding my identity in Christ, of building my life on God's acceptance, will often be a more ready acceptance of others. This contrasts sharply with the judgmental attitude that a more religious approach tends to foster. This is the subject of a remarkable book by Gregory Boyd, Repenting of Religion. 'Our fundamental sin,' Boyd suggests, 'is that we place ourselves in the position of God and divide the world between what we judge to be good and what we judge to be evil. And this judgement is the primary thing that keeps us from doing the central thing God created and saved us to do, namely, love like he loves.'[57]

Might we be more free to accept others, to love unconditionally, when we have, ourselves, encountered and received God's unconditional love?

54   Henri Nouwen, Life of the Beloved, New York, Crossroad, 1992

55   Ken Wilson, Mystically Wired: Exploring New Realms in Prayer, Nashville: Thomas Nelson, 2009

56   Ian Adams, Cave Refectory Road: monastic rhythms for contemporary living, Norwich: Canterbury Press, 2012

57   Gregory A Boyd, Repenting of Religion: Turning from Judgement to the Love of God, Grand Rapids: Baker Books, 2004

THE 'GOSPEL PRAYER'

American author J D Greear has developed in his own life an approach to faith that comes back, time and again, to this unconditional, unmerited acceptance by God. His 'Gospel Prayer' puts this into a simple, daily, personal liturgy:[58]

'If you are not where you should be spiritually,' Greear writes, 'the answer is not simply to get busier for Jesus. It is not just to get more radical in your devotion to God. It's not only to seek greater spiritual gifts or even to learn more about the Bible. It is to make your home in God's love given to you as a gift in Christ.'[59]

In Christ, there is nothing I can do
that would make you love me more
and nothing I have done
that makes you love me less.
Your presence and approval
are all I need for everlasting joy.
As you have been to me,
so I will be to others.
As I pray,
I'll measure your compassion
by the cross
and your power
by the resurrection.

58 J D Greear, Gospel: Recovering the Power that Made Christianity Revolutionary, Nashville: B and H, 2011

59 J D Greear, Gospel: Recovering the Power that Made Christianity Revolutionary, Nashville: B and H, 2011

"You want to be just like Jesus, because this is the way he made you. Like clay awaits a potter. Like canvas awaits a painter. Our lives long to be shaped by Jesus."

Go deeper into the Spring Harvest theme with Krish Kandiah

Available from EssentialChristian.com or your local Christian bookstore

essential christian

● ● ●

ENCOUNTERING GOOD NEWS: PETE GREIG

GOD SNEEZED

I gave up on God just before my eighteenth birthday. I had a broken heart from a broken relationship, disappointing A-level results and a fistful of unanswered prayers. I concluded that God didn't exist. Told him so regularly. Fortunately God didn't take my apostasy particularly seriously. Didn't question his own existence. Didn't give up on me. After several months of hide and seek, he jumped out of a Christmas card and nearly knocked me off my feet. It was a card from Brother Andrew with a verse from Isaiah 58: 'Your light will shine when you spend yourselves on behalf of the poor.' Bam. I walked out into that dark, December night in a haze. God had spoken.

That little epiphany propelled me 6,000 miles to Hong Kong where I found Jesus for real amongst former street-sleepers, Triad gang members and heroin addicts. In Jackie Pullinger's company, I learned that faith is an action before it's a creed. She explained to me that there's no point telling hungry people about the Bread of Life until we put rice in their bowls. I also learned that there's little point in putting rice in people's bowls if we never point them to the Bread of Life. The gospel marries mission and mercy, words with works, practical love with the prayerful variety too.

Three years later, God jumped out on me again - and I really must stress that I don't get ambushed like this often. I tend to be the guy left standing like a lemon when everyone else gets nuked by the Spirit. Imagine my surprise therefore, one night on some Portuguese cliffs, when I started shaking violently (note to self, cliff-tops = bad place for shaking, gently or otherwise). Then God gave me

a bewildering vision of an army of young people rising from the pages of a continental atlas. I didn't know what to do, so I started small. Became a youth worker in Chichester (which is very small if you know anything about the size of Chichester and the average age of its population). I didn't tell too many people about my vision in case they thought I was nuts. Ended up planting a couple of churches. One was great. The other folded.

Then, late one night in the first ever 24-7 prayer room, I had a third encounter with God. This one wasn't dramatic like a talking Christmas card or a shaking vision. It was less of a hijack, more of a 'Hi, Pete' whispered quietly. It was in a room where a bunch of us had started praying 24-7 and, amazingly, God had begun hanging out with us, wanting to chat. After a few weeks of this kind of night and day prayer, God must have sneezed because suddenly a beautiful virus began to spread around the world. Last time we counted, it had reached more than half the nations on earth. We've now been praying non-stop for well over a decade. Millions of people have been infected; encountering God's love in prayer rooms and then taking it out onto the streets, into schools, churches, workplaces. The good news has always been infectious. I guess I got it from a Christmas card, a bunch of Chinese ex-addicts and a community in Chichester that started seeking God and started sneezing.

I'm more and more convinced that encountering God is the heart and soul of Christian faith. Everything else - and I mean everything else - is peripheral to meeting with Jesus for yourself. There isn't a single major Bible character who didn't have some kind of life-defining encounter with God. Without that kind of experience, we will be plagued by insecurities, driven by a need to be loved instead of a knowledge of being loved. But just one encounter with God's love can change everything for everyone forever for good.[60]

---

60   Pete Greig is the founder of the 24-7 Prayer Movement, www.24-7prayer.com

Some questions to consider as you explore what it means for your identity to be found in Christ:

- **Who I am.** What does Scripture say about who I am in Christ? For an eye-opening list of references see encouragingBiblequotes.com/verses2a.html How can I more fully embrace this identity?

- **Who I am not.** What assumptions about identity do we need to leave behind? What are the alternative sources from which we draw identity? How does our encounter with Jesus challenge these other sources?

- **Coming to God in the stillness.** How does our rhythm of prayer impact on our identity? Can we remember who we are by remembering whose we are?

- **Loved to show love.** Blessed to be a blessing. How receiving from God is the source of giving to others.

EXERCISE: MAKE ROOM TO MEET GOD

Gerald May has developed a number of responses to the challenge of 'opening space in our lives for a greater awareness of God'. He has three suggestions for how to begin to create space:

- First, looking for spaces that occur normally in our lives that we might fill with other things such as turning on the television or making ourselves a drink. We can turn these into 'intentional' moments to stop and be still.

- Second, finding more regular, set-aside spaces during the day, even if quite short, that we can have as spaces just to be.

- Third, building in longer spaces for retreat, maybe even going away or taking a morning, a day or more, to have a prolonged period of quiet and reflection.[61]

EXERCISE: KNIT TOGETHER

How do we empower those we love to truly grasp their identity in Christ? Read Psalm 139 slowly. Ask yourself, do I believe this about myself? Now read it again and ask, do I believe this about my neighbour/daughter/colleague/enemy? If these words are true of them, how might you communicate this good news to them?

61   In Michael Schut, Simpler Living, Compassionate Life, New York: Morehouse, 1999

● ● ●

ENCOUNTERING GOOD NEWS: MELANIE CAVE

I don't like the news. It is usually so depressing. While driving in the car with the kids, I turn off the radio news because I don't want my young children to hear all the stories of war, murder and violence. The world is a scary, violent, oppressive, and lonely place for many people, so I crave good news. Hearing good news restores my faith in the goodness of people, in God, and in the world being a safe place. It makes me notice beauty and become more present in a moment with awe and gratitude. Good news gives me peace knowing things are 'as they should be'.

I grew up being taught the 'good news' that Jesus could save you from separation from God and from going to hell. Although that is indeed good news, it requires you to embrace an awful lot of bad news first: I'm a sinner. I've fallen short of God's perfect standards. I can't get out of this mess by myself. Only Jesus can pay the price for my sins by dying on the cross. However the good news is that Jesus loves me and has made a way for me.

Many of my friends don't believe all of that bad news, so in order for me to share that 'good news' I would first have to convince them of what a bad place they are in.

What strikes me about Jesus is that he doesn't spend much time talking to people about bad news. He says things like 'the kingdom of heaven is at hand'. 'Get up and walk!' 'Be healed!' 'Go and sin no more.' 'Daughter of Abraham, Your faith has made you well.'

Jesus is good news because he offers us his friendship that has the power to transform us:

I am secure in who I am; you can be yourself.
I am vulnerable; you can be too.
I am not afraid; you can live in peace.
I am your family; you can belong here.
I am your friend; you are not alone.
I tell the truth; you can believe me.
I have enough; you will be provided for.
I have needs; your love will make a difference to me.
I am just; I will treat you fairly.
I have been badly treated; you can challenge injustice.
I am strong; you can bring your troubles to me.
I am gentle; you can be broken here.
I am whole; you can be healed.
I know what to do; you can be restored.
I am full of joy; you can laugh.
I am not in a hurry; you can take your time.
I understand; you can be truly heard.
I love you; you can be loved.
I bring something special to the world; you can too.
All of my friends need this kind of friendship.

We all feel trapped by fears, pressures, unhelpful coping strategies, unhealthy and oppressive relationships, memories of wrongs done to us, and confusing and difficult emotions. My good news is that Jesus is my fearless liberator and healer. Jesus is changing me and releasing me from my fears and unhelpful coping strategies. Jesus is good news because he is provoking and changing the world as we see it into the world it should be: a place of justice, healing, restoration, love, understanding, beauty and joy. Each time I encounter Jesus, I experience his gentle and freeing power and I am reminded that I can bring justice, healing and beauty to the world. Whenever our lives show the impact of his friendship, we demonstrate the good news of Jesus.[62]

---

62   Melanie Cave is part of the leadership team at Open Heaven Church, Loughborough, and is mum to two young children.

SUMMARY

Because God is who he says he is in Jesus, so we are who God says we are: beautiful, broken, forgiven, invited. This is the anchor of our lives. What does it mean for you to inherit, in Christ, a whole new identity?

WHERE WE ARE:
BEING PRESENT TO
THE WORLD

'My whole life I have been complaining that my work was constantly interrupted, until I discovered that my interruptions were my work.'

Henri Nouwen[63]

In John 1:14 Jesus, the source, is described as 'moving into the neighbourhood'.[64] In Acts 17 Paul suggests to the people of Athens that every one of us, likewise, has been placed in a specific place and time. Every people group, he declares, has a God-given location.[65] And God has placed us where he's placed us for a reason: so that 'we might reach out and find him'.[66] We are where we are so that we can meet with Jesus. We are where we are to be good news.

LOCATION, LOCATION, LOCATION

This sense of 'place' runs right through the biblical narrative. Adam and Eve were 'placed' in the Garden; Abraham was called towards a new place; Moses was called to lead the people to a new land. Vocation, the call of God on our lives, is very often closely tied to location. The purpose of our lives might come to us in the form of a place. God calls us to be present to him and at the same time present to our world - aware of and engaged in the places he has for us.

'There is inevitably a social dimension to place; humans are placed in relationship, and in relationship they form and fashion places. Implacement is an on going, dynamic process, and, being cultural and social, it is also historical.'[67]

'Place' in this sense can have many meanings, just as we can answer the question 'where are we?' in a number of ways:

Where are we geographically? - our local setting
Where are we historically? - our position in time
Where are we socially? - our cultural context
Where are we globally? - our place in the human family

Being aware of and engaged in our 'location' in each of these dimensions is a vital part of our discipleship. What does good news mean in each of these contexts? What does Jesus have to say in all these places? How might a fuller engagement in these things deepen our sense of God's call?

63   Henri Nouwen, Reaching Out, New York: Doubleday, 1975

64   John 1:14, The Message

65   Acts 17:26

66   Acts 17:27

67   Craig Bartholomew, Where Mortals Dwell: A Christian View of Place for Today, Grand Rapids: Baker, 2011

THE THEOLOGY OF PLACE

Craig Bartholomew suggests that there are very strong theological grounds for connecting mission with location. Christian action, he suggests, always springs from loving, and loving springs from 'knowing'. We are more likely to act on behalf of a person or place when we truly know them - and that often comes from being in their locality. The followers of Christ are called to indwell the places God takes them to in the same way that Jesus found his place in Israel:

'Just as the presence of the Holy One among the Israelites was to permeate every aspect of their lives, so now this is how it is to be throughout the creation, as groups of followers live the life of the kingdom in their particular places.

Will we let our location impact our vocation? Will we hear God's call in those around us?'[68]

PEOPLE NEED PLACES

French intellectual Simone Weil wrote in 1949 that 'To be rooted is perhaps the most important and least recognised need of the human soul. It is one of the hardest to define. A human being has roots by virtue of his real, active, and natural participation in the life of his community which preserves in living shape certain particular treasures of the past, and certain particular expectations of the future.'[69] It is part of our humanity to be rooted in a given place or community, and part of our discipleship to express our faith in the context of that rootedness. God calls us to be fully present to the places in which we live.

68   Craig Bartholomew, Where Mortals Dwell: A Christian View of Place for Today, Grand Rapids: Baker, 2011

69   Simone Weil, The Need for Roots, London: Routledge, 1952, 2002

VENI VIDI VELCRO:
WE CAME, WE SAW, WE STUCK AROUND

There is a challenge here for the followers of Christ in the postmodern West. Is there a sense in which we have lost the capacity to be truly present to the places God has established us in? Do we inhabit certain places but fail to invest in them? Greg and Ruth Valerio confronted this challenge when they moved onto the Whyke Estate in Chichester, at the time a deprived and difficult neighbourhood.

RUTH VALERIO WRITES:

Eighteen years ago, fresh-faced and newly married, Greg and I moved onto the Whyke Estate in Chichester. It was a place that our church had invested into quite a bit over the years, running hugely popular summer play schemes and after-school clubs. A church plant had recently been started and we were one couple among those who volunteered to move there. A number of families lived on the edge of the estate and three households took the plunge and actually moved on. A classic working-class council estate, Whyke had all the problems that you would expect and we moved in, excited and expectant of the transformation that God would bring. However, I think God had other ideas and other lessons that he wanted to teach us and, after a few years which saw almost no one becoming a Christian, the church pulled the plug and interest turned elsewhere.

But we stayed. We actually lived there for six years before anything positive began to grow on Whyke. During that time the place got progressively worse and became the area that council tenants were dumped in when they got evicted from other estates. We were plagued by anti-social behaviour and racial violence, and twice friends of ours, on separate occasions, got beaten up walking home from our house in the evening. I was never too sure what we could do to get involved and people were suspicious of us because we were 'new' (our neighbour wouldn't let her daughter play in our garden because she thought we were from a cult), so I did the occasional half-hearted prayer walk and left it at that.

Then an enlightened local councillor saw what was happening to the estate and made enquiries of local residents to see who would be interested in forming a Community Association. I jumped at the chance and before long found myself co-chairing the Whyke Estate Community Association (WECA) and have done so ever since.

WECA has now been going for twelve years and the story of those twelve years would fill a book. But the result is something that I see every time I look out of my kitchen window or walk around the estate. We now have a community to be proud of: crime is at a minimum and the Green that the estate is built around has been transformed from a derelict place into a lovely area used by residents of all ages: walking their dogs, playing football, riding their bikes, sitting on the benches, admiring the community mosaic, having picnics, playing and generally enjoying themselves. The local housing authority has told us that we have changed the estate from a 'bad estate' into a 'good estate' and the proof is that people are now queuing up to live here, rather than queuing to get off!

No one has become a Christian yet, but it's still true to say that many people's lives have been changed by what we've achieved. I think particularly of a man who has got involved with WECA recently who is a long-term carer for his wife. Up until a few weeks ago he spent his days playing patience on the computer. Now he's spending his time designing posters for our summer fun day and writing a community newsletter and he's getting to know other people on the estate. And the church too is now beginning to pick up the mantle that it dropped all those years ago, looking at how it might begin to invest again in the life of the estate.

What I've learned is that there is no substitute for staying put. We live in a society that encourages us to move as we follow after work and climb the property ladder. It can be hard to resist that and the practicalities of life don't always make that possible, but I want to encourage you to recognise the benefits of staying in one place, putting your roots down in that community and not always chasing after the greener grass that seems to be somewhere else. Some of the best things in life take time to reach their fullness.

THE CHALLENGE OF CHANGE

Where mobility increases, the likelihood of finding this sense of rootedness decreases. Writing in the 1960s, pioneering urban planner Lewis Mumford was already warning that:

'Men are attached to places as they are attached to families and friends. When these loyalties come together, one has the most tenacious cement possible for human society. In the restless moving about of the past two centuries, this essential relationship between the human spirit and its background was derided, underestimated and sometimes overlooked. Where men shifted so easily, no cultural humus formed, no human tradition thickened.'[70]

Can we be truly at home in a hyper-mobile, globalised culture? To do so means, perhaps, to take more seriously the history and situation of the locations in which we serve. This was the experience of Bill Ind, Bishop of Truro from 1997 to 2008. Ind came into Cornwall as an outsider, but soon attracted a reputation as a 'champion and defender' of the Cornish region and identity. 'As our experience of the world becomes increasingly global,' he wrote, 'so it becomes increasingly important for us to know where we belong, where our home is'[71] His review of the ministry of the Anglican church in Cornwall, called 'People of God' emphasised the need for Christian mission to be fully localised; taking seriously the location and situation of those to whom it is addressed. Ind writes:

I believe people need to be helped to see that they are subjects in their own story and not, as they all too often do, as passive objects in someone else's. To use a phrase of Moltmann,

'Each of us has a history of our own with God.'[72]

Is there a place God has called you to, where being rooted is a vital part of your discipleship and mission? As you observe the lives of the people of that place, can you see ways in which they each have 'a history with God?' Are you ready for God to show where and how he is active already in your location?

THE RESPONSE: PLACEMAKING

Craig Bartholomew suggests that our response to the Bible's emphasis on 'place' should be to engage, as God's people, in 'placemaking' - co-operating with God in bringing a kingdom influence to the places in which we are set. He suggests that this will have a major impact on our attitude:

- To the cities God has called us to. A vision of urban life renewed by faith is vital to our mission in the cities of today.

- To our homes and gardens. Can we see homemaking and gardening as expressions of a godly sense of 'place'?

- To a whole range of everyday activities. From family life and friendship through public art to building and bird-watching.[73]

70   Lewis Mumford, The City in History, London: Secker and Warburg, 1961

71   Rt Rev Bill Ind, Towards a Theology of the People of God, www.trurocathedral.org.uk/PDF/PeopleofGod.pdf

72   Rt Rev Bill Ind, Towards a Theology of the People of God, www.trurocathedral.org.uk/PDF/PeopleofGod.pdf

73   Craig Bartholomew, Where Mortals Dwell: A Christian View of Place for Today, Grand Rapids: Baker, 2011

CREATION'S GROANING

The story of the Minet Country Park in Southall is a remarkable example of 'placemaking' in contemporary British culture. Dave Bookless tells this story of this transformational initiative:

My call to get involved in caring for creation in a practical way stemmed from my Christian faith. Back in 1989 I had a 'lightbulb' moment when for the first time it really dawned on me that my lifestyle was negatively affecting God's world, and that it was part of worshipping God to care for the planet. Moving to multiracial urban Southall in 1991 and working as a minister in two local churches there, I saw how a poor environment was a major factor in people's lack of hope for themselves or their locality. A report from the Southall Regeneration Partnership in 1998 concluded that there was a lack of greenery, open space, clean air and environmental awareness – all of which contribute to a lack of confidence and pride in the area.

On the edge of Southall lay a large plot of land, almost 90 acres in size, known locally as 'the Minet tip'.

It was an eyesore, used as an illegal fly-tipping site, for off-road motorbike scrambling, and as an unregulated car boot sale site.

The resultant litter – literally tons of it – and the quagmire of mud did nothing to inspire pride in the area. Walking around Minet amidst burned-out cars and fly-tipped rubbish I sensed God asking 'How do you think I feel about this place?' and I felt creation's groaning to be set free,[74] and a desire to seek the 'healing of the land'[75] in this place.

The hard work began with discovering who the site belonged to (Hillingdon Council) and who else had an interest in it. The groups included a cycling club, a football club and local residents. The local MP for Hayes and Harlington, John McDonnell, was hugely supportive and a consultative group was formed, including the Council. There were lots of different views: some people wanted to develop the site heavily for retail, leisure, even housing, but the local community were clear they wanted it clean, green and accessible.

I had known about A Rocha[76] for years - as a Christian charity doing nature conservation in Portugal and beyond - and had become increasingly involved myself, so it was natural to seek advice and prayer from them, and as the project developed, to seek to set it up under A Rocha's auspices. My wife and I had been inspired by seeing how A Rocha projects combine care for wildlife and habitats with care for people; integrating the social, environmental and spiritual aspects of the gospel, and we sought to do the same with A Rocha UK as it developed. So, whilst the Council knew it as 'Minet Country Park', to us it was part of a wider vision: 'A Rocha Living Waterways' seeking 'a greener, cleaner Southall and Hayes'.

74   Romans 8:19-22

75   2 Chronicles 7:14

76   www.arocha.org

The transformation of the Minet site took several years, with A Rocha UK providing ecological consultancy to the Council and acting as a bridge between them and the community – involving local people in clearing rubbish and planting trees. Once the works were completed, A Rocha continued to be involved in conservation, environmental education and community engagement. Since Minet opened as a new Country Park in 2003, we've had thousands of school children visit each year, and the park is used daily by hundreds of people to walk their dogs, kick footballs, cycle or just enjoy the ever-changing life of God's creation. As well as people, the wildlife enjoys it too – there are breeding Kingfishers and Woodpeckers, newts, dragonflies, foxes, voles and butterflies. Perhaps most significantly, it has become a sign of hope for local people. It is a story of 'good news' – that change is possible for even the most damaged and polluted areas, and for lives that may be hopeless and hurting too. In a small way, the story of Minet – of A Rocha Living Waterways – has become a sign of the kingdom – 'your will be done, on earth as in heaven'.[77]

---

77   An ordained Anglican minister, Dave Bookless is Advisor for Theology and churches to A Rocha International.

● ● ●

ENCOUNTERING GOOD NEWS: MARTIN GOLDSMITH

GLOBAL IS LOCAL

The world has changed amazingly. The local has become global: 400 years ago it took European missionaries two whole years to travel out to China or Japan. Usually 50 per cent died en-route. Even in the 1940s, missionaries to North West China had to walk the final 500 to 600 miles together with their children. They often needed over a year to get from Shanghai on the coast to their place of service. But today air travel makes light of distances – it is relatively cheap, quick and easy. Multitudes of British people go overseas as students, business people, Christian workers and tourists. Some of the Christian workers go overseas short-term in their gap year, between jobs or for a couple of weeks as part of their annual holidays. Others feel God calling them to longer-term service which allows for greater cultural adaptation and language learning. We all need to be careful not to export our western forms of Christian faith, worship or leadership.

It is equally true that multitudes of people from other ethnic backgrounds come to Britain both short-term and as long-term immigrants. They bring to us not only their various cultures and languages, but also their different religions – Hinduism, Islam, Buddhism etc. Globalisation challenges our churches and all of us as individuals. What makes the gospel 'good news' to people of these different backgrounds? How should we adjust our witness and church life to fit their needs?

The local has indeed become global. A blinkered British approach no longer fits the modern world. In our pluralistic secular or post-modern society our churches need the help of Christians from all ethnic backgrounds. Majority world Christians have so much to give us. And already in London they outnumber ethnic British church-goers, so their influence must grow.

Of course it is also true that British Christians with our long tradition of biblical faith and mission have much to give. Our understanding and practice of holistic mission emphasises not only the spiritual dimension, but also the developmental, social, environmental and ecological needs. Our churches are also often stronger in biblical teaching and exposition than those in Latin America or Africa.

This global vision is nothing new, but finds its roots throughout the Bible. The very beginning of the creation story underlines the need to look beyond the local to the global. God created everything and everybody, so he is Lord of all. His purposes reach out still to everything and everybody worldwide.

Israel was challenged to look back to its origins in the call of Abraham (Genesis 12), in which God promises that Abraham would be the 'father of many nations'. Although in the Old Testament God is called the 'God of Israel', he is also known as the 'God of all the earth'. In God's plan Israel was called to live in obedience to God's Law. Her life of holiness both as God's people together and as individual believers should demonstrate the reality, holiness and glory of her God. This would then attract the other nations to join Israel in faith and holy obedience.

Then in the New Testament Jesus sends his followers out into all the world. No longer should God's people consist only of Jews plus a few Gentile converts who joined the people of Israel and became like little Jews. Now Christians are sent out into all the world to make disciples of all nations. The church became international with both Jews and Gentiles as followers of Jesus as Messiah, Lord and saviour.

No longer merely local let's get out into our globalised world both in Britain and overseas for the glory of God.[78]

---

78   Martin Goldsmith is an Associate Lecturer at All Nations Christian College, Ware and author of Life's Tapestry and Beyond Beards and Burqas.

● ● ●

ENCOUNTERING
GOOD NEWS:
KAY MORGAN-GURR

For some, being 'present to the world' means acknowledging a situation of suffering or loss: accepting life 'as it is', not as we would wish it to be. Kay Morgan-Gurr, who has a long-term and increasing disability, reflects on what it means to encounter the good news in such a situation:

I have encountered Jesus all through my life, his presence is tangible to me most of the time. Other people have had a hand in showing me what it means to be good news, and I am so thankful for those people. I accepted this good news as being true at quite a young age and have continued to encounter Jesus in different ways as I have grown in faith - through school, being a nurse, and now as a children's evangelist and advisor on issues of disability and additional needs.

But now, with quite a history behind me and as I face a slowly worsening disability, how do I continue to encounter him, to speak out the good news and show that good news in my own actions? Some would say that my suffering shows this good news to be a lie, but I disagree. It is in my suffering as well as in joyful circumstances that I encounter Jesus, a man also acquainted with suffering but bringing hope where others cannot see hope. Even with this debilitating disease, I can speak to others about encountering Jesus and show him in the way I act and respond - choosing to give my complaints to him and not constantly burdening the people around me, choosing joy over fear; but also in being honest in the grief and pain that disability brings. That might sound flippant, as though it's an easy thing to do, but I acknowledge that it isn't.

This isn't just a 'warm and fuzzy' encounter with Jesus, it's a down to earth, heart-felt, teeth clenched and resolute encounter of the mind as well as the heart. This is strength pulled from the depths of the Bible where I read of his love and care. It's pulled from days where I will yell at God and tell him that things are not fair. It is only in my relationship with Jesus and the people I choose to be accountable to and learn from, that I can draw the strength to do the things God wants me to do.

Quite simply, without Jesus and his good news, I just couldn't cope.

Because of Jesus, I choose to smile. I am known for my smile. It isn't a stuck on 'Plastic Evan-jelly-grin'. It's born out of a life-time of growing with and encountering him in various situations and difficulties. Within those encounters I see that in the midst of everything, Jesus is truly good news. Because of Jesus I choose to carry on telling children this good news and showing them the joy of encountering Jesus for themselves. Because of Jesus I truly live.[79]

---

79   Kay Morgan-Gurr and her husband Steve are children's evangelists. Kay is General Director of Children Worldwide, an associate member of 'Churches for All' and an advisor to the Spring Harvest Theme Group.

ENCOUNTERING GOOD NEWS: THE BARONESS COX

Similarly, God's people in many settings around the world face hardship through persecution and oppression. Baroness Cox, who has highlighted the plight of such people groups for many years, insists that it is under such conditions of persecution that 'the good news of the gospel is most vividly demonstrated':

I love the word 'Enthusiasm'! As Christians we have a special reason to be enthusiastic because the real meaning of the word comes from the Greek 'entheos', meaning 'God in us'. What a concept! The God who loved us so much that he came to live and die as one of us is still eager to live with us, in us and through us.

When I was eleven years old I was confirmed in the Anglican Church. I still remember the Bible text the Bishop gave us from the book of Joshua: 'Have I not commanded you: be strong and of good courage; do not be afraid or dismayed for I your God am with you wherever you go.'[80] I must confess; I am often afraid and dismayed – but I then remember these words and try, in the words of a song called 'Pioneer' 'to go beyond my fear, to my own frontier'. We all have fears – but if we are open to God's calling, we may find ourselves going beyond those fears to frontiers where he wants us to be. They will be different for each of us. For me, they were choosing to be a nurse and then travelling further afield to visit people suffering persecution in Sudan, Nigeria (where there have already been many martyrs this year), the ancient Christian land of Armenia, India and Burma. I am often afraid, but when I go 'beyond my fear', I find wonderful people whom I would never have met if I had not gone to my own frontier. I find people who worship with joy even in the ruins of their destroyed churches; people who always love, even when they are persecuted; and I encounter modern miracles! Only time for one example of each:

A miracle of Grace: meet Ma Su in Burma, whose people are being attacked and killed by a ruthless military regime. Burmese soldiers shelled Ma Su's village; her house was burnt to cinders; she was shot in cold blood by a soldier. I met her sheltering in a friend's house, recovering from her wounds. When I asked her what she felt about the soldier who shot her, her reply was simple: 'I love him. The Bible says we should love our enemies. So of course I love him; he is my brother.'

A miracle of Protection: Armenia was the first nation to become Christian, in 301. But the people have suffered persecution over the centuries: 1.5 million Armenians were slaughtered by Turkey in a Genocide which began in 1915; then Stalin cut off a region of eastern Armenia called Nagorno Karabakh, relocating it within Azerbaijan. In the turbulent days of the break-up of the Soviet Union, the seven-million-strong Azerbaijans began ethnic cleansing the 150,000 Armenians of Karabakh, who tried valiantly to defend their land. David against Goliath.

But miracles abounded, such as the protection of a 13th century church building, which Azerbaijan tried to destroy with countless bombing raids from low-flying aircraft. Shells rained down directly onto the church – but a divine 'arm' always brushed them aside – and the only shell to penetrate this miraculous protection never exploded. It is embedded in the wall to this day.

The good news of the gospel is most vividly demonstrated under persecution, where the people worship with abundant joy even in the ruins of their churches. They are living testimonies to the biblical truth that 'God is a very present help in trouble' and to the dynamic power of 'Enthusiasm' – the never-failing good news that God will never abandon us.

A MIRACLE OF JOY

A 12-year-old Polish boy, in the horrors of the Warsaw Uprising, with bombs falling, tanks attacking, and people dying around him, wrote these words on a wall:

'I believe in the sun, even when I cannot see it;
I believe in love, even when I cannot feel it.'

That is real 'Enthusiasm': when you believe in the sun even on the dark days, when you cannot see it. And the good news is that our Enthusiasm is assured by a God who loves us, is always with us, and will never fail us.[81]

SUMMARY

No matter what our location; no matter what our circumstances, God has good news for us where we are. What does it mean for you to live out the love and grace of Christ in the places in which he has established you?

81   Caroline Cox, the Baroness Cox, is Founder and CEO of HART, the Humanitarian Aid Relief Trust

INTERLUDE: SURPRISED BY OXFORD[82]

Ultimately, being present to God and present to our world means finding our identity in him. It means letting Jesus - the Jesus of the Gospels, the Jesus offered to us in the story the Bible tells - tell us who we are. For some this is not an easy thing to do. We are used to establishing our own identity, to choosing just how we will construct our lives. We are used to being in charge. But change is possible. Surprised by Oxford tells the delightful and compelling story of just such a change: a modern-day conversion in the most unlikely of places.

Educated, cynical, radically feminist, determinedly secular, Carolyn Weber came to Oxford from the United States to pursue her studies in English Literature. Her memoir explores her reaction to being in the city of C S Lewis; to falling in love and, more importantly, to finding faith. This extract recounts how she was first intrigued by, and then drawn into, the epic story of God told in the Bible:

...St Mary's church, sitting resplendent in her shroud of architectural splendour, caught my eye. Her side door was open. I bet I can find a Bible in there, I reasoned, so I entered objectively. A sea of pews greeted me, each with a Bible and a hymnal tucked neatly inside every few feet. I could sit anywhere and have my pick, easily within reach. I thought at first that I could discreetly take one, or rather borrow one, and no one would notice. But then I thought better. Reading from a stolen Bible?

Something in that seemed a little coarse, even for a cynic like me. So instead I made my way to one of the back pews and sat down, irreverently crossing my ankles on the genuflecting cushion and resting my coffee on the handy little shelf for the welcome cards. I opened a Bible and began at the beginning, a very good place to start.

Before I really knew it, stealthily entering St Mary's by the side door with my morning coffee became something of a ritual for me. The church always owned a particular hush during the rush of a weekday. Sometimes I would return late in the evenings, too, after the Bodleian closed. I would step out of the chill into the candle glow. I enjoyed the peace, the solitude, the seeming transgression. Purchasing my own Bible seemed too much of a commitment, like getting married. Besides, the church was right across the street from my college, so, as they say, why purchase the cow when you can get the milk for free? I began coming more and more often.

Lilies in the field, a house with many mansions, the command to love one another; familiar echoes from an unfamiliar context. Seeds planted but nothing, really, I thought, to reap.

In this back pew I read the Bible steadily on borrowed pages. I devoured it, just as a best-selling book (which, coincidentally, it always has been). Even the long, monotonous lists. Even the really weird stuff, most of it so unbelievable as to only be true. I have to say I found it the most compelling

82   Carolyn Weber, Surprised by Oxford: A Memoir, Thomas Nelson, 2011

piece of creative non-fiction I had ever read. If I sat around for thousands of years, I could never come up with what it proposes, let alone with how intricately Genesis unfolds toward Revelation. That the supposed Creator of the entire universe became a vulnerable baby, born in straw, to a poor girl who claimed to be a virgin and who was betrothed to a guy probably scared out of his wits, but who stood by her anyway. It unwinds and recasts the world and our perception of it: that the Holy Grail is more likely to be the wooden cup of a carpenter than the golden chalice of kings.'[83]

Carolyn describes the Bible as 'the most compelling piece of creative non-fiction I had ever read'. How does this description sit alongside your own experience? Do you need to re-visit, with fresh eyes, the story of God?

ENDWORD: BE

Caring for the locations God has called us to, or simply placed us in; coming to terms with the bodies we inhabit, and their frailty; knowing courage in the face of oppression; discovering Jesus in one of the world's most intellectual centres - these are all diverse and dynamic examples of the same single idea: things change when we encounter Jesus today.

To 'Be' a good news Christian is to be transformed by the coming of Jesus; changed from within; given a new identity; discovering what it means to be present to God in the world. But it goes further. It is also to begin to imagine what the coming of Jesus might mean for the people and places around me: how might they, with their own special history, their own story with God, be so transformed?

What is the good news announcement for your location, for your context, for the people you connect with every day? The answer will in part be about identity, an outworking of who you are. But it will inevitably also, at some stage, be about communication, about words. The good news is not only carried in who you are and lived-out where you are: it lives also in what you say.

83   Carolyn Weber, Surprised by Oxford: A Memoir, Nashville: Thomas Nelson, 2011

IF SOMEONE ASKS ABOUT YOUR CHRISTIAN HOPE, ALWAYS BE READY TO EXPLAIN IT.

1 Peter 3:15

SAY

[THREE]

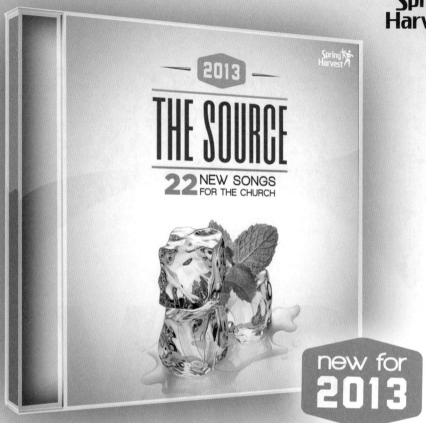

new for **2013**

THE SOURCE 22 NEW SONGS FOR THE CHURCH

22 new songs to inspire the church in worship

- 2 CDs featuring full band and acoustic arrangements
- Music scores for all the songs are available in the Spring Harvest Praise Digital and Printed songbook

Scan here to listen to track samples or buy online

Available from EssentialChristian.com or your local Christian bookstore

INTRO: 1 PETER 3:8-17

In 1 Peter 3:15, we are given the simple and much-quoted instruction: 'If someone asks about your Christian hope, always be ready to explain it.' The words fill the hearts of many believers with terror. Am I being asked to become an overnight apologist? To give a perfect explanation of the Christian faith to everyone I meet? Can I do it? Will I make the cut? What happens if I get something wrong?

But Peter's suggestion is much simpler than this. 'If someone asks you why you're hopeful, tell them,' he is saying. 'You have a story, don't be shy in sharing it.' This is not about apologetics at all. It is about authenticity. It is about honestly recounting who we are and why, and what has happened in our lives to convince us that Jesus is good news.

Peter's context is instructive. Verses 8-17 are all about the power of words, and of the actions that speak louder than them. 'Be tender hearted,' he says, 'When people insult you, don't insult them back, but bless them.' 'Don't let evil hijack your tongue. Don't let your lips lie.' 'And if someone asks you why - tell them.' 'And if in doubt', he says 'let your actions speak for you. Be humble. Seek peace. Do good. Do what is right.'

The picture is of a life in which actions and words work together; where what we say and what we do carry the same message. A life in which the good news comes through in both domains: when you do good without saying why and when you find the words to explain. The good news shapes our behaviour and our words, and sings the same God-song through both.

What are the challenges for us in lining up our lives with our words; in both living out and speaking out good news? Are there times, both personally and publicly, when the words we speak are out of sync with our behaviour? We want to ask what it means for the good news to infuse everything we say - personally and publicly; in the meanings of the words we speak, and the message of the lives we live. What are the key goals for this stage of our journey?

1. The first is understanding - we want to be equipped with an understanding of the good news, and of what it means to share it, that is liberating, life-affirming and filled with joy. We want to lose forever the guilt-driven, formulaic expressions of faith we have grown used to, and learn instead to know our own story; to tell God's story and to listen to the stories of others.

2. The second is practice - we want to identify practical, deliverable ways in which our communication, both personal and public, might change, to more fully reflect the good news of Jesus.

To do this, we will explore the two key areas in which our words carry the good news to others: the personal words with which we explain our faith to those close to us and the public spaces in which we make a louder noise, proclaiming good news to our culture.

"Does this stuff really work?" is probably the question to which most ordinary Christians in this country would like to hear a convincing answer.

PERSONAL WORDS: EXPLAINING GOOD NEWS

EXPLAINING NOT EXPOUNDING

At its heart Peter's encouragement to 'be ready to explain' is personal. There is a public dimension here - a task for the whole church to embrace - but there is also a much simpler, individual dimension. As you live out a Jesus-life, receiving God's unmerited favour and seeking to express it to others, how do you explain to those who ask you just how and why you have come to this place?

Many followers of Christ, despite being convinced for themselves that the choice they have made is the right one, are much less convinced or confident in explaining that choice to others. For a whole host of reasons, we find 'faith sharing' a difficult and sometimes terrifying experience. Alison Morgan suggests that this will often be rooted in the perceived hostility or indifference of our culture.

'We live in a culture which dents and knocks our confidence as Christians,' she writes, 'And so

It's expressed in different ways, but whether people are asking us to help them to know how to find ways of reaching out to others, or to deepen their relationship with God, or to pray for healing, what they really mean is perhaps just this: can we actually have confidence in this ancient faith of ours? Do we really have something which people out there need and want - or not?'[84]

The honesty of this analysis is refreshing. Instead of getting hung up on a guilt-trip around our reluctance or inadequacies as Christ's heralds, perhaps we should address this lack of confidence head-on. Perhaps a deeper awareness and fuller understanding of our own journey with Christ would help us to come to a place of greater confidence? Morgan goes on to suggest that knowing and telling our own story is one significant response to this confidence deficit:

'... we can answer through experience,' she suggests, 'it has changed me; let it change you. We each have our own story to tell, and it is important that we tell it; the good news is not just something we believe but something we live - it changes us, and therein lies its power, its attractiveness, its uniqueness. We are not those odd people with a peculiarly antiquated sense of how to have a good time on Sunday morning, we are - or should be - living witnesses to the power of God to bring healing and transformation to ordinary lives.'[85]

84 Alison Morgan, The Word on the Wind: Renewing Confidence in the Gospel, Oxford: Monarch Books, 2011

85 Alison Morgan, The Word on the Wind: Renewing Confidence in the Gospel, Oxford: Monarch Books, 2011

If you were trying to share with a friend or colleague your account of something that had actually happened - your story of real events; real changes - might you be less intimidated than on those occasions when you have tried to communicate 'the whole gospel'? Might your fear of missing something out, or getting something wrong, or simply being misunderstood, evaporate if you only ever talked about the parts of the gospel that you have actually experienced - the things you have seen and heard, tested and tasted? Could you abandon the need to be a religious expert and simply be a faithful witness instead? This is about explaining, not expounding; about hanging out, not haranguing. It is about answering the questions of those you are in relationship with - finding genuine answers to match their genuine questions. The first evangelistic sermon of the New Testament church was preached by Peter on the day of Pentecost - and it only happened because people were asking what was going on. Is it too simple to adopt a rule of life that says:

- When they ask, answer.
- When they don't ask, live in such a way that soon they will.

Brennan Manning suggests: 'What the world longs for from the Christian faith is the witness of men and women daring enough to be different, humble enough to make mistakes, wild enough to be burnt in the fire of love, real enough to make others see how unreal they are.'[86]

Honesty. Authenticity. Reality. Aren't these the safest place to stand in sharing good news with those around you?

A PERSONAL EASTER?

This suggestion that you can best share the love and truth of Christ by telling your own story, authentically relating how Christ has changed your life, equally applies to the gospel's core events - the death and resurrection of Jesus. Instead of describing what in theory you think has happened as a result of this event, why not explore, and explain, the impact these events have had on you. What has it meant for you to bring to the cross your burdens, your anxieties, your shame? What does it mean in your life that Christ is not dead but risen? It is surprising that we talk so often of the Easter events and yet struggle to connect them with our own life journey. Can you find your personal connections? Are you ready to share these with others?

86   Brennan Manning, Souvenirs of Solitude: Finding Rest in Abba's Embrace, Colorado Springs: NavPress, 2009

RELAX!

Carl Medearis suggests that our churches need a massive transformation, from forced efforts at evangelism to the simple, relaxed reality of sharing with friends.

'Relax,' he writes. 'Enjoy your friends. Enjoy their company along with the company of Jesus. Point him out, freely, without fear or intimidation. You're not responsible to sell him to them. You're simply saying what you've seen. You're not the judge. You're the witness.[87]

Tim Chester has explored this model of 'relaxed sharing' by highlighting the vital role of common meals in the life and ministry of Jesus - the kingdom explored around the table of the everyday. In A Meal With Jesus: Discovering Grace, Community and Mission Around the Table,[88] he cites Robert Karris, who concludes that throughout Luke's Gospel in particular, 'Jesus is either going to a meal, at a meal, or coming from a meal'.

'There are three ways the New Testament completes the sentence, 'the son of Man came...', Chester writes, 'The Son of Man came not to be served but to serve, and to give his life as a ransom for many' (Mark 10:45); 'The Son of Man came to seek and save the lost' (Luke 19:10); 'The Son of Man has come eating and drinking...' (Luke 7:34).

The first two are statements of purpose. Why did Jesus come? He came to serve, to give his life as a ransom, to seek and save the lost. The third is a statement of method. How did Jesus come? He came eating and drinking.

Jesus spent his time eating and drinking – a lot of his time. He was a party animal.

His mission strategy was a long meal, stretching into the evening. He did evangelism and discipleship round a table with some grilled fish, a loaf of bread and a pitcher of wine.'[89] Can you re-imagine the process of evangelism through this paradigm of sharing meals and telling stories?

Such an approach will require easy, positive relationships of mutual respect with people who choose not to be called Christian. 'Those who avoid the contamination of sinners' Chester writes, 'are like the Pharisees. Those who earn the label "friend of sinners" are like their saviour.'[90]

---

87   Carl Medearis, Speaking of Jesus: the Art of Not-Evangelism, Colorado Springs: David C Cook, 2011

88   Tim Chester, A Meal With Jesus: Discovering Grace, Community and Mission Around the Table, Wheaton: Crossway, 2011

89   Tim Chester, A Meal With Jesus: Discovering Grace, Community and Mission Around the Table, Wheaton: Crossway, 2011

90   Tim Chester, A Meal With Jesus: Discovering Grace, Community and Mission Around the Table, Wheaton: Crossway, 2011

WHAT PERSONAL EVANGELISM IS NOT

The model of conversational, story-based faith-sharing in the context of relaxed relationship helps us to establish what evangelism isn't. In this setting it is not:

- **A series of clichés,** platitudes or motivational catch-phrases. Real communication, linked to real events and experiences, doesn't need to fall back on such short-cuts.

- **The whole gospel.** Faith-sharing in a relationship is part of a process, not all of it. Who knows what other initiatives and resources God is going to call on?

- **A task whose success or failure** is on your shoulders. Your responsibility is to be authentic, truthful, sensitive, compassionate; to tell your story well. The rest, according to Jesus, is the work of the Holy Spirit.

- **A theology exam.** Nobody is waiting to pass or fail you.

- **A combination lock** where only one specific sequence works.

WHAT PERSONAL EVANGELISM MAY WELL BE

- **An invitation to journey.** If there comes a context in which you are encouraging someone to take the next step in their journey with Jesus, it is always just that - one step. Effective discipleship is not counted in scalps but in growth and fruitfulness. What is the next thing that God might be inviting this person to do?

- **A link in a chain.** You will never be the only voice an individual hears. Even if there's no one else about, the Trinity make three, so you're at least one of four. More likely one of many, many more.

- **A challenge to know and tell your own story.** It's surprising how difficult it can be to answer the simplest of questions. How has the encounter with Jesus impacted your life?

- **An integration of words and actions.** You may well value words above actions, but in the end those who see and hear you will draw from both.

- **An expression of dialogue.** The best conversations are mutually edifying. Genuine exchange always, in some measure, goes both ways.

- **Grounded in listening.** Listen early, speak late is a good rule. Better still; listen early, listen again, then listen to make sure you've heard well, then consider speaking a possible option, unless more listening would be more helpful.

- **A kingdom operation,** shaped by the widest possible view of God's purposes. What makes your words good news? To whom?

THE PARTICULARITY OF JESUS

There is a corollary to the above that it is important not to miss. We have looked at the idea of Jesus as the Source of our gospel, and there is an important sense in which a conversation, in order to qualify as Christian discourse, in order to contribute to discipleship, must carry, somehow, the Jesus story. 'Christianity is universal in that it welcomes everybody,' Timothy Keller writes, 'but it is also particular in its confession that Jesus is Lord, and culture and ethnicity (or whatever other identity) are not.'[91]

The story of Jesus is a particular story, rooted in historical events. Both Scripture and history show that people are transformed by their contact with this story. Are our conversations about our longings for a better world, or about how the Jesus story promises one? Are we simply distributing good advice, or are we pointing to Jesus? As Tom Wright insists, no matter how broad and wide our vision of the kingdom, it only is the kingdom when it centres on the king, and especially on the unique events of his death and resurrection:

'Somehow, Jesus's death was seen by Jesus himself, and then by those who told and ultimately wrote his story, as the ultimate means by which God's kingdom was established. The crucifixion was the shocking answer to the prayer that God's kingdom would come on earth as in heaven. It was the ultimate Exodus event through which the tyrant was defeated, God's people were set free and given their fresh vocation, and God's presence was established in their midst in a completely new way for which the Temple itself was just an advance pointer. That is why, in John's Gospel, the 'glory of God' - with all the echoes of the anticipated return of YHWH to Zion - is revealed in and through Jesus, throughout his public career, in the 'signs' he performed, but fully and finally as he is 'lifted up' on the cross.'[92]

It is in this context that the challenge to respond, the place of repentance, the call to change, all come in. It is as our conversation encounters Jesus that we can legitimately ask for a response. We are inviting those we love to respond to Jesus - not to us, not to our church or denomination, not to our religion. It is in responding to Jesus that they will find life - let's not make it harder by putting other things in the way!

The way in which the early church worked out their telling of the story is fascinating. C H Dodd, in his book on The Apostolic Preaching and its Developments[93] traces the kerygma — the preaching — of the disciples in the book of Acts. He analyses the message recorded in different missional contexts. They tell the story of Jesus: his Messiahship (for Jewish audiences), life, death, resurrection, exaltation, and his return to consummate the new age. There's an emphasis on the promise of the Holy Spirit, and the need to respond in repentance, belief and baptism. But they tell the Jesus story, and relate it to the story of their hearers.

JESUS' STORY IN JESUS' WORDS

One intriguing suggestion that has been made is to tell the story of Jesus by using the words of Jesus. This involves reading and knowing the Gospels and commending to your friends and contacts the magnificence of the words, actions, responses and relationships of Jesus. Rather than pass on to your friends your words about Jesus, why not introduce them to Jesus' words about them?

91   Tim Keller, Center Church: Doing Balanced, Gospel-Centred Ministry in Your City, Grand Rapids: Zondervan, 2012

92   N T Wright, Simply Jesus: A New Vision Of Who He Was, What He Did, And Why it Matters, London: Harper Collins, 2011

93   C H Dodd, The Apostolic Preaching and its Developments, Hodder & Stoughton, 1967

FOUR STORIES

Laurence Singlehurst has suggested another approach to enabling Christians to be more confident in sharing their faith. Most of us, he suggests, have favourite stories or incidents from the life and ministry of Jesus - the passages in the Gospels we come back to time and time again; the stories that have most shaped us. Why not choose just four of these stories - your own personal 'four Gospels'. Knowing which four stories have most touched you, become familiar with them; read their texts and let them be the basis of your Jesus story. Let these be the stories you tell, sharing in simplicity and authenticity the reasons they grip you and the dent they have made in your life.

PROVOCATION

What provokes the question? Peter's assumption in the verses we looked at earlier is that something in the life of the believer will provoke a question for which an answer is needed. If there is no intrigue, what needs explaining? If you have no hope, why would anyone ask you to account for it? What kinds of questions does your life provoke?

THE POWER OF LISTENING

Scripture is filled with incidents in which listening is important: Daniel at the Court of Nebuchadnezzar in Daniel 2, Paul in Athens in Acts 17, Jesus with Nicodemus in John 3, with the Samaritan woman in John 4 are just a few strong examples. Take a look at these passages, or at other encounters, especially in the ministry of Jesus. Highlight in your Bible the places where listening matters. Ask yourself how you can listen early and speak late.

CONTEXT AND CONNECTION

What makes the good news good? The answer is to do with where and how it 'lands'. To the sick, healing is good news. To the lonely, friendship. To the guilty, forgiveness. It is good news because God is good, but it becomes good news to us when it connects. What are the different contexts and conditions in which the people surrounding you live? What connections do these throw up with the Jesus story? Where that connection exists, good news is possible.

● ● ●
ENCOUNTERING GOOD
NEWS: CRIS ROGERS

Sometimes the biggest challenge facing us is not what we have to say about our faith, but what people have already assumed about it. Part of our task in explaining what we believe and why may be to unravel false perceptions about belief. Cris Rogers describes his own experience of this challenge:

One of the biggest tasks we have in sharing our faith is unravelling all the misunderstandings people have about faith, Jesus and the church. I recently had someone ask me if I thought it was odd that Jesus was always going round walking on water, surely this must prove that Jesus wasn't real. I had to start by explaining that as far as we know he only walked on water once, not that that negates how strange a thing that was, but that it also wasn't the only reason to judge Jesus, he did much more than that.

Whilst at university I had a Saturday job working for a high-street chain selling cameras. Every Saturday I would head down to the store and try to make as many sales as I could. The big problem was that this was right at the start of the digital era and every week there was a new product to try to get your head around.

Each week I had to fake knowing information to try to make the sale. The reality is that without knowing the product I couldn't sell the product - but when I trusted that this product really worked I could sell more and more each week. The early church lived out this rebellious good news in such a way that they communicated that they trusted it. Their lives backed up the message of good news, which made their words so much more powerful.

I recently found myself having a conversation with a woman who was amazed to find out that I was a church leader. We had met at a day conference on sexuality and I had found myself sitting next to her. A number of times during our conversation she said I was just too young to be a vicar, and that if churches had young leaders like me they all would be full which we all know isn't really true. Using this opportunity I was able to ask her why she thought people would go to church if they had young leaders and then asked her if she knew why people even went to church. With a blank look on her face I started to tell her all about how I had come to faith after reading the Gospels and that the Jesus I found in the pages of the Bible was so compelling that I couldn't help wanting to give my life to his mission. We talked at some length about how the message of Jesus really was good news and how the church often has let this powerful message down.

After quite a long time chatting she proudly declared that if this was all true and the gospel really was good news, then everyone really needed to hear it. I simply responded with 'Amen'.

How can we become more confident in SAYING the good news? The answer is we need to get to know Jesus and his good news better. We need to spend time in his presence and then we will have something to say.

TOP TIPS FOR SHARING YOUR FAITH

• **We need to be talking to Jesus** - asking him daily for opportunities and then going out into the day wide open to them. Often we have our eyes closed to opportunities given to us.

• **Be willing speak about Jesus** and not necessarily about church or religion. Many people are put off from church and Christianity because of how they see it portrayed in the media, but they are intrigued about Jesus and what he said and did.

• **Don't try to win arguments or be judgmental** towards the responses people give. No one will be argued into believing in Jesus' good news but they can be loved and engaged into conversation - and into the kingdom!

• **Gossip Jesus.** It's maybe good to start a conversation by offering to pray for someone or giving them some wisdom on an issue, but make sure you end up by bringing them to Jesus. It's easy without thinking to share religion with people without sharing Jesus. Jesus is the one who brings us hope, friendship and support so make sure it's him you lead people to.[94]

94   Cris Rogers is Vicar of All Hallows' Church, Bow, London.
Before Bow, Cris worked in Birmingham as a youth worker and
then led Soul Survivor Church in Harrow.

● ● ●

ENCOUNTERING GOOD NEWS: JAMES HAMILTON

Last weekend we invited some good friends of ours round for a Chinese takeaway. The general consensus was to do that sharing thing, where we order a selection of dishes and all tuck in. I'm sure you do this as well. I ordered my usual – crispy shredded beef in Peking sauce, and then I don't even remember what else we had. As usual, Amber Chinese Takeaway had come up trumps - it was delicious. After our friends had left, I realised that when I went round to collect it, they had under-charged me by £10. They were very busy and so must have read £17.40 instead of £27.40. I have to be honest and say that my first reaction was... Result!

I told my wife Cally about our stroke of good fortune. I should have seen it coming. I should have just kept it to myself. Why did I tell Cally? You know the rest. She sent me round to the takeaway at 5pm opening time the next day with a ten pound note in hand. But I have to say, this was one of the best £10 I had ever (sort of) spent. The look on the guy's face behind the counter was priceless. Let alone the two guys waiting for their orders, who looked up from their newspapers jaws open. I handed over the £10 and left the shop. It was then that a very warm, proud and somewhat self-righteous feeling overcame me. What good news I had brought to the Chinese takeaway industry that day. When I got home I was expecting the red carpet, the medal,

the congratulations and kiss that my honesty deserved. Surprisingly, I was greeted by a question. 'Did you tell them you were a Christian?'
'Ah.'

What a question; would you have? After all this was a comparatively extraordinary thing to do in this day and age. Had I missed a great opportunity to share the good news? Probably. As I thought more about my incredible gesture of kindness and honesty, the reality hit me. As a Christian, I am good news, I have good news and I must share good news. This good news is worth more than £10. Yes, maybe I did miss an opportunity to share my faith in the Chinese takeaway but what Jesus has done for me and who Jesus is in my life is worth sharing in every situation, not just the extraordinary moments that life throws up. In Proverbs 3:5 we are reminded to acknowledge our Creator and Lord in all our ways. 'In all your ways acknowledge him'.

Through my ministry in producing short Bible-based films for schools and churches, I want to be used by God to make a lasting difference, to excite kids about the Bible, to help them understand more about Jesus. But if I am honest, after all that Jesus has done for me in my life and the lives of my friends and family, there has to be more. What I really want to do is devote my whole life, not just 'what I do', but who I am, to be an act of worship to the one who paid the price for my sins and eternal life. In all my ways I want to acknowledge him. Not just when I think I have done a good thing.

By the way, guess what we are having next Saturday night...[95]

---

95   James Hamilton www.reliveresources.co.uk

● ● ●

ENCOUNTERING GOOD NEWS: EL McKENNEY

Good news for me was and is a simple yet profound experience: love. I guess to put it into perspective I should fill in some of the background. My childhood was pretty much as broken as it can get: a father who abandon a disabled mother to bring up three children alone. For us it was an aspiration to even touch the poverty line, let alone live above it. Yet church, from as young as I can remember, was part of my life. Through my childhood eyes though, words and actions told two different stories. I never heard the loving Father spoken of; my own had abandoned me. I never saw the caring body; only the frowns when I wore scuffed shoes. My early experience of church was a bad one, and it pushed me away. As Brennan Manning said:

'The greatest single cause of atheism in the world today is Christians who acknowledge Jesus with their lips and walk out the door and deny him by their life style. That is what an unbelieving world simply finds unbelievable.'[96]

Until as a teenager, through a youth group, I met Christians that really took an interest, cared about me, loved me. Through their genuine interest and encouragement I began to see, for the first time, what love looked like.

A change of location, a new period in life and mixing with new people led to me making friends with a group of local Christians. If it hadn't been for their friendship, kindness, patience and their love, I would never have understood what love is. It was a big learning curve, and still is at times, but without that experience I would never have been able to reach the point of understanding that meant I could accept the love that my heavenly Father has for me. I had grown up knowing about love but it wasn't until I experienced love that I understood the good news. Love for me was being invited to the cinema, to hang out, to do the simple things. Love isn't a set of rules and judgements. We love because He loved us (1 John 4:19).

As Veggie Tales put it 'When you love your neighbour, loving means lending a hand' or as Jesus put it 'Love your neighbour as yourself'.[97] Today love hasn't changed: it still is thinking of others, being the person that holds the door, who gives up their seat, saying yes when you really want to say no, buying an extra coffee, being a friend, and going out of our way. But it's also about praying hard that some of that love rubs off, and those love actions lead to an opportunity to explain; to introduce the good news, the greatest love of all.[98] A love that died so we can live.[99]

---

96   Brennan Manning, via DC Talk

97   Matthew 22:39

98   John 3:16

99   El McKenney is an early years' educator and a regular under-fives' leader at Spring Harvest

PUBLIC SPACES: PROCLAIMING GOOD NEWS

'Nero did not throw Christians to the lions because they confessed that 'Jesus is Lord of my heart.' It was rather because they confessed that 'Jesus is Lord of all,' meaning that Jesus was Lord even over the realm Caesar claimed as his domain of absolute authority.'[100]

Michael F Bird

PUBLIC IMAGE LTD

There are two dangers in limiting the scope of faith-sharing to the personal. The first is that by doing so, we implicitly accept and endorse the enlightenment assumption that faith only belongs in the private sphere - that it has no role in public life. We thus rob public discourse of the vital contribution that our faith can make. The second is that we will sell short the gospel itself, making it a matter for me but not for the universe. This is the flipside of the call to root our understanding of the gospel in the impact God has had on our own journey. Your story

is a way-in to God's story, but it neither contains nor exhausts it. God is always bigger than my experience of him. As Alison Morgan insists:

'...we need to be sure that we are talking not just about our own experiences, something that worked for me but might not work for you, but about something universal; something much bigger, something into which our individual stories fit like pieces of a jigsaw. To do this, we need to be able to understand and respond with confidence to some of the intellectual challenges our culture throws up to the gospel, to know why and how it is that we genuinely have something powerful and true to offer. We need to be able not just to encourage those around us with our real life stories, but also to help them through the tangle of voices which press in on all of us, voices which offer illusory and ultimately unsatisfactory answers to the big questions of human existence.'[101]

The gospel then, is not only about private faith but also universal truth - it belongs not only in personal words but also in public spaces. Alongside our personal, meal-time encounters, there is a wider 'conversation' taking place in our culture. This is the conversation of the media: newspapers and magazines and television programmes; of the arts; of education both formal and informal; of seminars and preaching; even of the local pub or street corner. In recent years it has become the conversation of the internet, of web sites, blogs and social networks. It is fuelled by the transmission of ideas, the exchange of opinions, the forming of worldviews and the shaping of minds. It is a conversation to which faith has a vital and significant contribution to make.

'Our culture offers us a myriad of false stories rooted in superficial worldviews,' Scot McKnight suggests, 'These stories, more often than not, refuse entrance to the gospel story or reshape that gospel story or seek overtly to destroy that that story. ... What are those stories?

100   Michael F Bird, Introducing Paul: The Man, His Mission and His Message, Downers Grove: IVP, 2008

101   Alison Morgan, The Word on the Wind: Renewing Confidence in the Gospel, Oxford: Monarch Books, 2011

Individualism
The story that 'I' am the centre of the universe

Consumerism
The story that I am what I own

Nationalism
The story that my nation is God's nation

Moral relativism
The story that we can't know what is
universally good

Scientific naturalism
The story that all that matters is matter

New Age
The story that we are gods

Postmodern tribalism
The story that all that matters is what my small
group thinks

Salvation by therapy
The story that I can come to my full human potential
through inner exploration[102]

To each of these stories, the story of Jesus offers
itself in conversation, not as a belligerent enemy
but as a respectful dialogue-partner. Are there ways
in which we can more fully and fruitfully engage in
this realm of public truth?

102   Scot McKnight, The King Jesus Gospel: The Original Good
News Revisited, Grand Rapids: Zondervan, 2011

SCIENTIFIC NATURALISM

NEW

AGE

POSTMODERN
TRIBALISM

SALVATION

BY

THERAPY

96

FAITH SEEKING UNDERSTANDING

In his last book published as Archbishop of Canterbury, Rowan Williams insists that the primary response of Christians to public issues should be a desire to seek understanding - far more than to tell others how to behave. He writes:

'About 100 years ago, a very distinguished Anglican theologian by the name of John Neville Figgis, a priest of the Community of the Resurrection in Yorkshire, wrote about how the church should be seeking to shape public opinion. And by that he meant, first and foremost, shaping public opinion within its own boundaries. The church ought to be a place where people were educating one another about civic questions and human dignity, where people were educating and being educated about liberty, responsibility, the creation of a sustainable human environment. And Figgis said that the significance of trying to shape public opinion within the church was something quite different from an institutional programme on the part of the church to impose its vision on everybody else.'[103]

Our problem, all too often, is that we don't know deeply enough how the story of Jesus does impact on these diverse areas. If we think the Jesus narrative is no more than the answer to the question 'how can I get to heaven?' then we will have nothing to say until that question is asked. But what if the story is wider? What if there is a Jesus answer to other questions, questions like...

Can a paedophile ever be forgiven?
Is there ever a justification for slavery?
Is beauty a physical or emotional attribute?
Will we ever explore the stars?
Can renewable energies save us?
Does pumpkin soup matter?
Does 2 + 2 always equal 4?

... Then life might get a little more interesting. And God might call some of us not just to be aware of these questions, but to dive deeply into them; to wrestle with them and with Scripture and, inspired by God's Spirit, to begin to suggest some answers. Theology is the work of the people of God, not of the academic elite. What is your church thinking about this month?

IT'S NOT WHAT YOU SAY...

It's the way that you say it. An important aspect of public truth is that its audience is undefined and unpredictable, and might respond quite differently to our expectations of them. In the end it's not what is said but what is heard that matters. The contrast is captured by the comments of Eric Metaxas, formerly of the Veggie Tales, when he was asked to address the National Prayer Breakfast in Washington DC, in 2012.

'I realized everything I had rejected about God was actually not God. It was just dead religion. It was phoniness. It was people who go to church and do not show the love of Jesus. It was people who know the Bible and use it as a weapon. People who don't practice what they preach. People who are indifferent to the poor and suffering. People who use religion as a way to exclude others from their group. People who use religion as a way to judge others. I had rejected that, but guess what? Jesus had also rejected that. He had railed against that and called people to real life and real faith. Jesus was and is the enemy of dead religion. He came to deliver us from that.'[104]

What is important here is that the impressions of the young Metaxas may well not have been justified at all - the people he had perceived to be narrow, unloving and judgmental may have in fact been open, loving and kind - but that wasn't what he heard. Do our public words sometimes make such a perception possible, even when our

103   Rowan Williams, Faith in the Public Square, London: Bloomsbury Continuum, 2012

104   Eric Metaxas, National Prayer Breakfast, Washington DC, Feb 2nd, 2012

true behaviour doesn't warrant it? Is there a place for greater humility in our public proclamations; for a position of gentle self-awareness? Can we begin more of our sermons, more of our articles, more of our blog-posts with the phrase 'I may be wrong, but...'

FACEBOOK FALLOUT?

The new world of social networks is a particular challenge in this area; the challenge of communicating authentically in a connected world, where words once thought private become public. Not only are we at times caught off-guard because things we thought we were saying behind closed doors have become the equivalent of broadcast news, but there is also a marked sense in which the world of blogs and networks encourages dissent. Christians in particular seem capable of speaking to one another via the web in a way that they would never do either a) face to face or b) in more formal print media. Blogs, status posts, comments and counter-comments seem to lend themselves to polarisation, and at two o'clock in the morning polarisation is only one step away from verbal abuse -which in turn lives next door to libel.

Do we need to take a rain-check on the 'gospel' that the church, collectively, is preaching on the net? Is there anything we can do to spice it with grace?

BOTH BARRELS

Preaching itself, still a vital aspect of the life of our churches, has an important account to give in this area. It is one of the few forms of discourse remaining in our culture that is at one and the same time both private and public. Private because it is often addressed to the believing community in a relatively closed setting; because it is often received by the individual as a form of intimate speech. But public because it is proclaimed, amplified, intentionally projected to a wide audience; because few if any of our churches these days are so closed that only the faithful are listening; because many, many sermons find their way to YouTube... Preaching is an opportunity to develop truth that is both personal and public; it is an opportunity to demonstrate the relevance of the Jesus story to every sphere: but it can also be an opportunity to be badly misunderstood if we do not recognise its role as public discourse. Again, it's not always what I said that matters so much as what is heard.

Your church may genuinely not be homophobic, your pastor may genuinely not hate sinners, your creeds and doctrines may genuinely not be narrow and judgmental. But a two-minute YouTube clip can convince a public audience otherwise - and it may be an audience exponentially larger than the one that was present at the time.

Can the words we use week by week change the conversation we are having with our culture? How might our approach to preaching change if we understood that we have two audiences – the faithful who sit close to us and a broader public, listening-in from a distance?

● ● ●

ENCOUNTERING GOOD NEWS: ARFON JONES

COMMON LANGUAGE; COMMON CONNECTION

In 1995, Arfon Jones had been serving as General Secretary of the Evangelical Alliance (EA) in Wales for over five years, and he was a regular speaker at Spring Harvest in its Pwllheli days. At that time an Evangelical Working Group had been set up to work on the revision of the New Welsh Bible, and Arfon was co-ordinating the group.

It was then that God started stirring and awakening a new vision in Arfon's heart. As a first language Welsh-speaker he felt God was calling him to a very specific task – to help his fellow Cymry (Welsh-speakers) encounter Jesus. There was a dynamic renewal of interest in Welsh language and culture, Welsh medium education was growing and more and more people of all ages were re-discovering the language and wanting to learn it. But at the same time the churches were very much in decline with ageing congregations, and there was a sense of hopelessness. Young people felt that the church was irrelevant, and that the Bible was boring, confusing and very hard to understand. Adult learners of the language found the Bible difficult because they were learning spoken Welsh not literary Welsh.

In the midst of all this Arfon recalls, 'I had a growing sense of restlessness, and yet at the same time it was as if God was engraving the word "hope" on my heart. And of course, Jesus is the source of that hope! How was this new generation of Welsh-speakers going to encounter that hope?'

The work of revising the New Welsh Translation was crucially important, but its language and ethos was that of the highest literary quality – similar to an English translation such as the RSV. The only other translation available in Welsh was the one popularly known as 'the William Morgan Translation' (1588). So Arfon started working on a colloquial, 'easy to read' translation of the New Testament in popular Welsh. If Welsh young people were to encounter Jesus then the Bible would have to be accessible.

In 1999 Arfon stepped down from his role with EA, and Gobaith i Gymru (Hope for Wales) was set up as an evangelistic trust with the specific aim of reaching the Welsh-speaking community. Among its various activities, beibl.net,[105] as it became known, was a key project. The vision had to do with the medium as well as the message. On March 1st, 2002, the website was launched, with the New Testament translation in popular spoken Welsh.

Arfon comments, 'The New Testament was put on the internet because I thought it would be the preferred medium for young people. The medium's flexibility was also appealing because the translation could easily be revised. But two things happened – people started asking when it was going to be available in print, and also when some Old Testament books would be available.' Since then Arfon has been working on translating the Hebrew Scriptures, and recently the whole Bible became available on the website.

So what's next? 'It's just the beginning' says Arfon. 'The beibl.net website is far more than just the translation. There are all kinds of resources available for download – discipleship resources, Bible studies and meditations, sketches, resources for schools, podcasts and much more. The translation itself is also now available on various mobile phone apps. Phase 2 is to develop further initiatives that encourage people to read the Bible and help people understand what God is saying. Our heart cry is "Come Lord Jesus" It's the Holy Spirit that "earths" any encounter with Jesus and transforms lives to become good news.'

'There's definitely a sense that God is up to something in the Welsh-speaking scene There are encouraging signs of new life. But there is far more to do, and many more people to be reached.'

● ● ●
ENCOUNTERING GOOD
NEWS: JOEL EDWARDS

It happened somewhere in the mist of my teenage years. It may have been about 1968 but I can still recall the impact when my pastor trumpeted the words of Isaiah 61:1, 'The Spirit of the Lord is upon me because he has anointed me to preach good news to the poor. He has sent me to bind up the broken-hearted, to proclaim freedom to the captives.'

Of course he had no intention of applying this messianic passage to me. I was just another person in a crowded church. But somehow I identified with that text and its New Testament equivalent (Luke 4:18) so profoundly that he may just as well have been talking directly to me.

More than any other single passage of Scripture, it has influenced and shaped my understanding of what God in Christ is about in the world, and what it means to align ourselves with the good news mission of Jesus.

The idea of God's good news in Jesus has been like a homing signal since that time. In the complexities of our theological debates, the political wrangling of Christian leadership and the tricky business of relating our living faith to a multi-dimensional world, the conviction of a good news God has been a central theme for me.

This is not about social engineering. For me, good news began with a radical and dramatic conversion and an incredible sense of forgiveness when I was about eleven. And that journey with the good news Jesus sustained me through Bible college, eleven years as a probation officer and over 20 years as a senior staff member in the Evangelical Alliance UK. But it has also been pivotal in all of my dealings with both the sceptical and sympathetic people with whom I have worked in community, policing or the human rights field.

And supremely, Jesus the liberator of the oppressed has been our guiding light in my current work in Micah Challenge[106] as we have worked to educate and mobilise Christians to respond to the poor and hold governments responsible for their promises to the 1.4 billion people who still experience the sin of extreme poverty in our world.

The good news about Jesus in this arena is a reminder to the church and our world that God has a comprehensive concern about human flourishing uniquely expressed in the cross and generously applied in freedom from oppression and injustice. Good news is about human well-being and no definition of Jesus' mission, which avoids the imperative of biblical and social justice, can completely claim to be good news.

In over 30 years in Christian leadership, perhaps my greatest opportunity to explore the magnificence of this passage which has meant so much to me over the years came recently in the filming of an educational documentary, The Jesus Agenda.[107] The documentary was an opportunity to visit four continents talking with theologians, evangelists, politicians and community activists about Jesus' statement about his good news manifesto and what that means for the church and our political leaders in the 21st century.

One thing above all that emerged from the exploration: the good news is as powerful today as it was when Jesus spoke it out in Nazareth or when I first heard it in north London.[108]

---

106   www.micahchallenge.org

107   www.thejesusagenda.org

108   Joel Edwards is Director of Micah Challenge International

● ● ●

ENCOUNTERING GOOD
///
NEWS: NICK HARDING
///

Meeting Jesus personally for the first time was a revelation, an entirely life-changing encounter, and a source of complaint. I had grown up in a Christian home and loving church, and I couldn't understand why no-one had told me what a radical experience meeting with Christ would be. Of course, on reflection, I know they had, and I also know that the Holy Spirit had been at work...but at the time it all came as something of a shock.

This stunning encounter with Jesus gave me many things, but the main thing was, and is, hope. The hope of real forgiveness, a future with Christ, and a lifetime of being in his presence, gave me the direction and drive that I needed. As a fairly shy and unsure child I was transformed by the truth that Jesus loved me for who I was, and was willing to change me to be the messenger he wants me to be. Of course, that's still a process I'm going through a few decades later, but the hope of perfection remains.

For me the good news is always about hope, and sharing that hope with the poor, the confused, the weak and the undervalued has always been my aim. So I try to be hope for people who need someone to support them, and share the hope of Christ with those who are in dark places or losing their way. That's why I believe in sharing the good news directly with children and young people, some of whom live pressured lives where hope is placed in all the wrong aspirations, and failure to meet those false targets means despair. Others grow up in situations of grinding poverty, neglect and abuse where there is apparently no hope at all. In Christ there is a new and life-changing hope, one that will carry them through life with vision and purpose whatever challenges there are to face or mountains there are to climb. But they need to hear this good news of hope in Jesus.

The longer I try to live out the good news the more I realise that I don't know much. I have lots more to learn about the grace of God and the hope he gives me. But I do know that living the good news through grace, kindness and forgiveness speaks just as loudly as preaching. This is an area that always requires more prayer and commitment. I am a 'work in progress', working towards becoming more the hope that Jesus offers in my attitudes, dealings with others, and lifestyle. It's a challenge... but there is hope.[109]

SUMMARY
/////////////////////////

Communication is at the heart of community, and the words we use matter. Both personally and publicly, we can speak words that, like the words of Jesus, speak life to those who hear us. What does it mean for you to explain and proclaim the gospel as good news?

109   Nick Harding is the Children's Ministry Adviser for the Anglican Diocese of Southwell and Nottingham, a lay member of the General Synod and a Trustee of Scripture Union. He was the inaugural Chair of the Trustees of Godly Play UK.

INTERLUDE: ISA IN IRAQ

I love this account from Carl Medearis of an incident in his ongoing work with Muslims in the Middle East. There is something intriguing and significant about this encounter, where it is the sharing of the stories of Jesus - not the unwrapping of what we believe about him - that opens doors. Are there others, not in the Middle East but right here in our towns and cities who, unknown to us, have a deep longing to hear the stories of Jesus? Might they be waiting, even now, to meet the Jesus of the stories? Medearis writes:

'Sometimes those we think are 'furthest away' have a greater appreciation for Jesus than those of us 'nearest' to him. I was staying with friends at a hotel in Basra, Iraq, in the spring of 2003. While there, we managed to attract the curiosity of the hotel staff. They were curious about this team of international people staying at their hotel. Since a war was well under way, they were all the more intrigued because we weren't wearing camouflage and toting M4 carbines. During the day, out in the streets, we had given out all of our texts - Arabic translations of the Gospel of Luke. We were checking in for another day and as we stood in the lobby near the front desk, the hospitality manager leaned across the counter and looked at me.

'Why have you come here?' he asked in English, 'Are you with the American army?'
'No', I said, 'we followed Jesus to Basra, so we are trying to find out what he is doing here.'
He took in his breath with a hiss. 'Isa?' he asked, using the Muslims' name for Jesus. 'Isa is in Basra?'
'We think so,' my friend Samir said, 'and he wants us to help out in any way we can.'

The manager made something like a gasping sound and snatched the phone of the cradle. He rattled off a quick sentence in Arabic, hung up, and came around to the front of the desk. 'If you please,' he said, 'stay right here. I know you must be very busy, but I had to call my brother. He loves to hear about Isa.'

Samir and I looked at each other. Isa was in Basra after all.

Within a few seconds, three other men joined us, all in their twenties and thirties, wearing the dark blue uniform suit of the hotel staff. For a moment I wondered if they were going to ask us to leave. Then, one of the men, with black hair and a thickening moustache, rushed forward and shook my hand. He moved on down the line, shaking hands vigorously, his eyes lit up like candles.

'You know about Isa?' he asked, returning to me.
'Yes' I said in Arabic, 'We followed him here.'
'Oh my.' His hands shot to his face.
'Let me tell you something,' he went on. 'When I was a young boy, a man came through our city, and he was telling stories about Isa to the people.'
The rest of the group and the hotel staff moved closer, listening intently.

'When this man left, he gave my father a cassette tape with recordings of the stories of Isa, the miracles and teachings of Isa, the people he talked to, and how he lived.'

'Wow,' I said.
'Every night, for ten years, my father would play the tape for me and my brothers and sisters. He played it until the tape did not work any more.' He stopped for a second, caught his breath. 'I love these stories of Isa, and I miss them.'

'Well,' I said, 'We...'
He cut me off, excited. 'I have heard, from my father and the old men of the city, they say there are books, sacred books, ancient books that tell the stories of Isa, as they happened, by the friends of Isa. Is this true?'
'Yes,' I said, 'and as a matter of fact, we have been giving them out all day.'

He almost fainted. I could see his face colour, then pale, then colour again. He was vibrating with excitement. 'Oh please,' he said as he gripped my hand, 'you must find one for me. You must give me one. I have to have one.'

'All right,' I said, and turned toward the elevator, 'I'll see if I've got one left.'

As I rode the elevator up to my room, I realised I was nearly shaking from the same excitement.
I almost never see someone who cares about the stories of Jesus like this man did. It's rare. Back in the States, sermons and teachings often revolve around a doctrine, theology, and how to live a more fulfilling life. We seem to have forgotten the power and the humility and the sheer genius of Jesus, his vibrancy and his compassion. To the man in the hotel, Jesus was the ultimate folk hero, a person of mystery and influence, and he was ecstatic about finding the stories of Jesus again. He was thirsty...

I tore my room apart. I ripped open my suitcases and threw my clothes all over the room. ... Finally, after scrabbling around in my luggage like a miner digging for ore, I found one: a Gospel of Luke. In Arabic, the title was something like 'the Gospel of Luke, a follower of Jesus.' I snatched it, raced out of the room and rushed for the lobby.

I will never forget his face when I handed it to him. With tears on his cheeks, he held it reverently, lifted it to his forehead, and closed his eyes. He lowered it to his lips, gave it a kiss, and then slowly opened it to look at the print. He lovingly ran his fingers over the pages, and then bolted for the lobby desk. He picked up the phone, dialled rapidly, and spoke even faster. When he hung up, he looked at me and said, 'I had to call my father; he will know if these are the same stories of Isa as I heard before.'

We waited for a few minutes, and after some time an aging Iraqi man showed up - grey beard and all. He looked at us a little suspiciously at first and made his way over to his son, who was literally popping up and down with excitement.

'Papa" he said, 'these men have come here because they are followers of Isa. I told them about the stories of Isa on the tape, and asked them if they had heard of the writings of the stories, and they gave me one of them.'

The old man came closer, picked up the Gospel, and lifted it to his face. He read the title, thumbed through the pages, pausing to read here and there, and then he stopped, lifted the book to his lips and kissed it, tears in the corners of his eyes. 'Yes,' he said, 'this is it. These are the stories of Isa.' He wrung our hands, hugging us to his body, so grateful that he shook.'[110]

How does this encounter challenge your understanding of evangelism? In such a context, encountering such people, what would Jesus do?

110   Carl Medearis, Speaking of Jesus: the Art of Not-Evangelism, Colorado Springs: David C Cook, 2011

ENDWORD
COMPELLING HOPE

It is significant that Peter links the explaining of the gospel not to truth, but to hope. The news we share becomes good news when it points to possibilities others may have missed; when it speaks a word of living hope to the very real dilemmas we face as individuals, as families and as a culture. Perhaps part of the challenge is not so much to explain better as to hope more - to seek God for such a compelling hope for our own lives and for our planet that our every conversation will be spiced with new possibilities. At a time in history where a severe and global economic crisis has taken its place alongside huge environmental challenges and the presence or possibility of war in many places, hope is a commodity in short supply. Might it not be for such a time as this that God has brought us into his kingdom?

For an intelligent and insightful exploration of the challenges facing our culture, see Hope in Troubled Times[111] by Bob Goudzwaard, Mark Vander Vennen, and David Van Heemst. Lead author Goudzwaard is a Professor of Economics and former member of the Dutch Parliament. His purpose is to examine major issues facing our world and to ask how the Christian community might speak into them with the voice of hope - recognising that the choice between hope and cynicism is fundamental in our times. Hope in Troubled Times is an excellent example of the process by which faith can move from the private religious sphere to the realms of public truth. Not least, it acknowledges that hard work is required in the process. Deep thinking and deep prayer, in this sense, belong together: hearts that seek after God and minds willing to be transformed.

111   Bob Goudzwaard, Mark Vander Vennen, and David Van Heemst, Hope in Troubled Times: A New Vision for Confronting Global Crises, Grand Rapids: Baker Academic, 2007

THE ONLY ONES AMONG YOU WHO WILL BE TRULY HAPPY ARE THOSE WHO WILL HAVE SOUGHT AND FOUND HOW TO SERVE.

Albert Schweitzer

'The only ones among you who will be truly happy are those who will have sought and found how to serve.' Albert Schweitzer [112]

WHAT ARE THE KEY GOALS FOR THIS FINAL STAGE OF OUR JOURNEY?

'Engagement with Jesus must move us beyond being spectators to being participants. If we wish to become like him, we must learn to participate in Jesus, actively applying him and his teachings to our lives. We cannot be disinterested spectators when it comes to following Jesus. In fact, in the encounters described in the New Testament, the desire of people to remain neutral observers is in a sense the real sin (eg, the rich young ruler and Pilate). The Pharisees want to 'check Jesus out', objectify him, line him up against their understandings of the faith, and because of this they are judged for their hardness of heart, for holding themselves back from what God is doing in Jesus. It is those who allow Jesus to get into their hearts and heads who end up entering the kingdom.'[113]

INTRO: 1 CORINTHIANS 13:1-7

These words are probably chosen more often as a wedding reading than any other passage in Scripture. And it is right that they should be - Paul's portrait of love is as challenging and inviting to a couple starting out together as to anyone else. But to leave these words in the realm of romantic love, to limit them to marriage, would be a disaster. This is not love as it should be lived by a couple in their life together. It is love as it should be lived by all of us. Love as God intends it to be lived by every human being he has made. This is love that can change the world.

At the heart of the passage is the assertion that 'if I don't love others, I am nothing'. Without love - lived out, embodied, acted upon - there can be no good news. It is as we love that we both experience and extend the good news of God's kingdom. The challenge, then, beyond all we are called to BE, beyond all we might SAY, is this: what will we DO to bring the good news to our world?

We have already touched on this in asserting, in Part Three, that our behaviour speaks a message that is louder than our words, and that both must act in chorus if we want to be heard. But here we must go further. Loving action does not only speak of the kingdom, it actually brings the kingdom. Love does not just carry a message. Love changes the world. We want to look at the actions that go beyond communicating who God is to actually bring something of who God is into our world: actions that are in themselves the answer to Jesus' prayer, that God's kingdom might come 'on Earth as in Heaven'.

We will explore such actions in two domains. In the practical, we will ask what a life marked by love might look like. How do my actions in the world move forward, or hold back, God's coming kingdom? What does it mean for each of us to live a love-soaked life? In the prophetic we want to ask how the actions we take now can point to God's coming kingdom. What can we do now that shows beyond doubt that another world is coming? Can we live, today, as if that world were here already? How much of the 'not yet' of the kingdom can be moved, through our actions, into the now?

God is calling a people not only to speak out good news, but to bring good news in their actions and choices: to show a broken world, hungry for healing, that resurrection has begun. To announce the good news of the revolution God has already started. As Leonardo Da Vince is credited with saying:

'Knowing is not enough, we must apply. Being willing is not enough, we must do.'[114]

112   Cited in Alan Hirsch and Lance ford, Right Here Right Now: Everyday Mission for Everyday People, Grand Rapids: Baker Books, 2011

113   Alan Hirsch and Lance Ford, Right Here Right Now: Everyday Mission for Everyday People, Grand Rapids: Baker Books, 2011

114   Leonardo Da Vinci, cited in Simon Guillebaud, Dangerously Alive: African Adventures of Faith Under Fire, Oxford: Monarch, 2011

PRACTICAL: MARKED BY LOVE

'Genuine biblical faith in God takes us to a place that is beyond intellectual assent and a mere collation of correct ideas about God. It transforms us into carriers and transmitters of the very love that rescued us in the first place.' Alan Hirsch[115]

The clear distinctive of the life and ministry of Jesus was love: whoever Jesus encountered, in whatever circumstances, he left them knowing they had met love. In his death as well as in his life, he took the love he has for us to its greatest extreme. Jesus' life was marked by love. And if we are to live as his followers, if he truly is our source - then we too will be marked by love.

What does this mean?
- It means that 'neighbour love', drawing on the command to 'love our neighbour as ourselves', will be the centrepiece of our lifestyle.

- It means we will be distinctive. The mark of love is the distinctive by which Jesus wants his followers to be known.

- It means that our ultimate goal is to love. All other goals - to grow our churches, for example, or to see people respond to the gospel - must take second place to our desire to love.

This last assertion is important when we consider mission, and the idea of sharing the good news. If love is our ultimate goal, then we will never be in a situation in which we show love to someone just so that they will accept the faith. Rather than loving people in order to win them, we are called to win people in order that we might love them. Love is the goal - love given; love received, love shared and celebrated. And if we serve, we do so to demonstrate love: serving others is the outward

expression of the inward reality of love. This gives an excellent clue as to how we should pray if we want to be more missional; to be more effective in faith-sharing; to more fully grasp and proclaim the good news; to be more like Jesus: Pray that you will love more.

JESUS-SHAPED MISSION

'The heart of discipleship is unfettered adherence to Christ, his message, and his values. He makes absolute claim to our loyalty and allegiance.'
Alan Hirsch [116]

Practical love is responsive to God's love - we become conduits of the love that has captured us. Good news, to be good news, HAS to be worked out in practical love. Before exploring what this motivation of love is, it is important to understand what it is not. Specifically, the life of practical love we are called to live:

- is NOT a guilt-response to poverty and suffering. We may have cause to reflect on our own lifestyles, we may need to repent of our selfishness, but true love values a person for who they are not for the function they might fulfil in assuaging our guilt.

- is NOT by an opportunity to further exercise our ego. There is a danger that our love for those in need might come too closely attached to our own neediness. It is possible to appear to be feeding the hungry when in fact we are feeding our own need to be needed.

- is NOT an outworking of our own Messiah complex. The differences that often become apparent between those being loved and those who do the loving can turn the lover into a rescuing hero. But we are not the answer - Jesus is. There is only one Messiah, and I'm not it.

None of us is perfect, and our motivations will often be mixed: this shouldn't stop us from loving. But our goal is to love as Jesus loves, and ultimately

---

115   Alan Hirsch and Lance Ford, Right Here Right Now: Everyday Mission for Everyday People, Grand Rapids: Baker Books, 2011

116   Alan Hirsch and Lance Ford, Right Here Right Now: Everyday Mission for Everyday People, Grand Rapids: Baker Books, 2011

this means shaking off some of these temptations. The call to Christ-like love is, by definition, a call to unconditional love. We would do well to heed the advice of the Apostle Paul, who urged his friends in Philippi to have 'the same attitude as Jesus' - characterised, in one of the earliest worship liturgies on record, as self-emptying love:

'He had equal status with God but didn't think so much of himself that he had to cling to the advantages of that status no matter what. Not at all. When the time came, he set aside the privileges of deity and took on the status of a slave, became human. Having become human, he stayed human. It was an incredibly humbling process. He didn't claim special privileges. Instead, he lived a selfless, obedient life and then died a selfless, obedient death - and the worst kind of death at that - a crucifixion.'[117]

The words that complete this remarkable first-century poem reinforce the place of this self-emptying love in our lives:

'Because of that obedience, God lifted him high and honoured him far beyond anyone or anything, ever, so that all created beings in heaven and on earth—even those long ago dead and buried—will bow in worship before this Jesus Christ, and call out in praise that he is the Master of all, to the glorious honour of God the Father.'[118]

It is because of love that we worship Jesus. He has neither crushed us with his power nor cajoled us with his words: rather, he has conquered us by love. The hearts that give to him their worship, the tongues that sing out his name, are those whom he has wooed and won. So too, in whatever sense God calls us to win others, it is by love that we will win them. There is a direct link between the life and example of Jesus and the life we are called to as those who honour his name. As Tom Wright has said:

'Here is the heart of it. The more you tell the story of Jesus and pray for his Spirit, the more you discover what the church should be doing in the present time.'[119]

117   Philippians 2:5-8, The Message

118   Philippians 2:9-11, The Message

119   Tom Wright, How God Became King: Getting to the Heart of the Gospels, London: SPCK, 2012

CARE AND COMMUNITY IN THE EARLY CHURCH[120]

There is a beautiful prayer by Clement of Rome, written around AD100. He prayed, 'We beg you Lord to help and defend us. Deliver the oppressed, pity the insignificant, raise the fallen, show yourself to the needy, heal the sick, bring back those who have gone astray, feed the hungry, lift up the weak, take off the prisoners' chains. May every nation come to know that you alone are God, that Jesus Christ is your child, that we are your people, the sheep that you pasture.'

These inspiring words highlight a feature of the early church that was one of their most notable: that enmeshed in their desire for people to know God was an amazing amount of social care that they undertook as they cared for the needs of the poor, both within and without their communities. This feature was even commented on by the pagan emperor, Julian, in the middle of the fourth century, who commented that, 'the impious Galileans (i.e. Christians) support not merely their own poor, but ours as well'.

The early church was birthed into a period of massive social unrest and instability. Although the might of Rome was at its zenith as the church was starting, by the end of the second century it was beginning to crumble and Roman power was becoming increasingly erratic. The majority of the population of the Roman Empire bore the brunt of heavy taxation to pay for the increasing demands of an army needed to maintain boundary control, and divisions in society were growing alarmingly. Demand for food was getting bigger, but available land was diminishing as the Empire took land away from the peasants and gave it to retiring army officials with no farming knowledge. Poverty and hardship was thus the lot for a great many people; a condition that was exacerbated by numerous natural disasters in those first centuries.

Christians, of course, were not immune to any of this and they also had to face the consequences of their being a minority group who refused to acknowledge anyone as Lord except Jesus Christ, suffering intense persecution as a result. To be a Christian, therefore, often meant accepting great social and economic instability and insecurity.

---

120   Ruth Valerio, taken from D. Batson, The Treasure Chest of the Early Christians: Faith, Care and Community from the Apostolic Age to Constantine the Great, Eerdmans, 2001

The response of the Christian community to this situation was nothing short of astounding as they set up systems to look after as many people as they could. Tertullian (one of the key leaders of the second century) gave this description: 'Though we have our treasure chest, it is not made up of purchase-money, as of a religion that has its price. On the monthly day, if he likes, each puts in a small donation; but only if it be his pleasure, and if he is able: for there is no compulsion; all is voluntary. These gifts are, as it were, piety's deposit fund. For they are not taken thence and spent on feasts, and drinking-bouts, and eating-houses, but to support and bury poor people, to supply the wants of boys and girls destitute of means and parents, and of old persons confined now to the house; such, too, as have suffered shipwreck; and is if there happens to be any in the mines, or banished to the islands, or shut up in the prisons, for nothing but their fidelity to the cause of God's church, they become the nurselings of their confession.'

Inevitably, there was not unanimity in how Christians responded to the needs of others. Writing a little earlier than Tertullian, Cyprian of Carthage lamented how different things were to the very first descriptions of the early church. As he said, 'Then they used to give up for sale houses and estates; and that they might lay up for themselves treasures in heaven, presented to the apostles the price of them, to be distributed for the use of the poor. But now we do not even give the tenths from our patrimony; and while our Lord bids us sell, we rather buy and increase our store. Thus the vigour of our faith dwindled away from us; thus has the strength of believers grown weak.' It is perhaps encouraging to know that comparisons with the church of Acts have been taking place for such a long time!

Nonetheless, the way that the church in those first centuries was right at the front of social care should inspire us as we look at the needs in our own society and today's world. Aristides, in AD 125, said about the Christians that, 'If there is among them a man that is poor and needy, and they have not an abundance of necessaries, they fast two or three days that they may supply the needy with their necessary food.' May such generosity of life be found in us too.

EXERCISE: CHARLIE CHAPLIN'S CANE

Church Actually: Rediscovering the Brilliance of God's Plan was published by Spring Harvest in 2012 as a further exploration of the event theme of that year. One particular exercise in it points towards this suggestion that for our mission to be Jesus-shaped, we will somehow need to look a lot like Jesus:

'Imagine arriving in a seaside town for a weekend break. You've been busy and are tired, and you fall asleep on the train until the jolt of arrival wakes you. You rub your eyes, gather your belongings and disembark from the train. But as you set off on foot to find your hotel, you wonder if you might still be dreaming. You pass Charlie Chaplin in the ticket hall, and then again, miraculously, holding the door for you as you leave. Just outside the Post Office he waddles by again and outside your hotel there are four Charlies unloading gear from a white Transit van. You think you may have crossed into a parallel universe, until you realise you have in fact walked into a lookalike convention. You work this out slowly in your tiredness, but in the end the moustaches, the little hats, the walking canes give it away. Why would everybody be dressed like Charlie Chaplin if not for such a convention? Why would people walk like Charlie and behave like Charlie unless looking like Charlie was their thing?

Now imagine a second weekend break, a few months later. Again you are tired. Again you fall asleep on the train. Again the jolt wakes you and you rouse yourself and set off for your hotel. This time, though, the convention is a gathering of Christians. It is followers of Christ, not Charlie Chaplin lookalikes, who have taken over the town. So here's the question: how would you know?

What is it that sets Christians apart, that identifies them, and what is it supposed to be? The answer to the first question might range from stickers and sandals to rainbow guitar straps. The answer to the second is simpler - it's supposed to be love. Servant love, in the manner of Jesus, is intended to be the mark of the Christian community: as clear and recognisable as Charlie Chaplin's cane and walk. Catholic theologians have called this the 'option for the poor' - it is the weighting of the church's mission towards those most in need. Because kindness moves towards those who are suffering; because the mission of God is to free humans from all that distorts his image in them; the calibration of the church around a 'kindness revolution' is good news for the poor.'[121]

121   Gerard Kelly, Church Actually: Rediscovering the Brilliance of God's Plan, Oxford: Lion Hudson, 2011

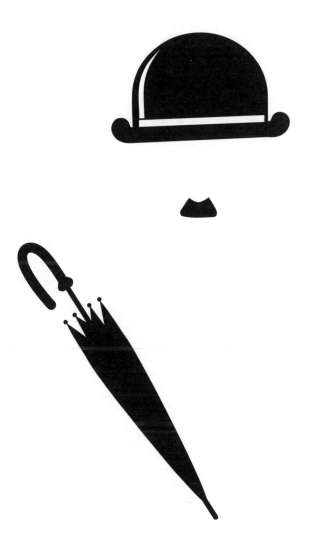

SEE, HEAR, LOVE

In many ways this practical, Jesus-shaped love begins with seeing. We often talk of 'seeing the need', but perhaps we should talk more of 'seeing the person'. We will never walk in love towards those who are invisible to us; it is those we see who move our hearts. Can we ask God to broaden our vision, to include those we presently don't see, and to deepen our vision so that we see more closely those around us? What might it mean for you to see your community and your world through the eyes of love?

Equally, the love of Christ might come to heal our deafness. Are there those whose cries we do not hear; whose pleas fall on our deaf ears; whose stories we haven't listened to; whose names we do not even know? What might it mean for you to listen more closely to those around you? To give real time to hearing the stories of others? Might you begin by asking them their name?

Throughout Scripture, the 'doing' of God's works sits alongside the call to worship him. In Matthew 22:34-40 the 'Greatest Commandment' implicitly asks that our love for God be matched by our love for others. In Matthew 25:31-46, the parable of the sheep and goats makes practical love - love expressed in specific, measurable actions - the key criteria against which the people of God are judged. The letter of James[122] similarly declares as empty, words of faith that are not matched by works. The prophets of the Old Testament, not least Amos,[123] call the people of God away from a life of worship unmatched by loving action, back to the life of transforming love God first called them to. In all these examples, the 'DO' of the good news is placed alongside, or even above, the 'SAY'.

---

122   See any or all of James 1:22-25, 2:1-13, 2:14-26, 3:13-18, 5:1-6

123   See Amos 2:6-8, 5:10-15, 8:4-6

OUT OF AFRICA

Bob Geldof, Bono, Bill and Melinda Gates - there is a long list of celebrities for whom the plight of Africa's poor has been decisive in making major life changes. For many Christians, too, this has been the case. Simon Guillebaud is a modern-day missionary adventurer for whom the people of Burundi have become precious friends. The author of More Than Conquerers, Guillebaud has also told, in Dangerously Alive, the story of his call to Africa, and a decision to embody the love of Christ in radical action. The story of Paul, an orphan rescued from intense poverty, illustrates Guillebaud's understanding of practical love:

'Today Freddy came round with his wife, baby and new addition to the family, Paul, to have an early Christmas lunch with us. Freddy now once again lives by faith with no salary. Despite having virtually nothing itself, he recently came across Paul, lying in the sun, half-dead with malaria, and so he took him in as unofficial second son. Paul had just the best day of his life. This emaciated little boy stuffed his face next to me for an hour, never having seen so much food before. His story is that he recently watched his mum and dad die of tuberculosis in one of the refugee camps. His aunt then took him in, but he was constantly beaten, so he fled with his brother who subsequently got blown up by a grenade in the nearby market. That's where Freddy found him, lying in the shell of a burnt-out car - his new 'home'.

After our feast, I put him on a swing in the garden and pushed him several times. He started giggling and then laughing in innocent abandon, exhibiting a beautiful, rotten-toothed smile spread from ear to ear. In front of everyone, I suddenly choked and nearly burst into tears. How could such a simple thing as a swing ride bring such unadulterated joy?

What on earth do I mean when I say that my life has been 'tough'? I have much to learn. Freddy and I praised God for Paul, as we saw his life as an illustration of grace. He has gone from being plucked out of the gutter to feasting like a king, adopted into a new and loving family.

I returned last week from three weeks' preaching in the USA. I met a lot of wonderful, hospitable people and thoroughly enjoyed it. But the contrast with Burundi was hard to reconcile. Travelling between the two, via the UK, has been a culture shock both ways. We live on the same planet, yet most of us don't seem to really care enough for the hundreds of thousands of dying Pauls (who are not a statistic to God, even if they are to us) to be prepared to make any significant lifestyle sacrifices. We invest so much of our time, energy and resources in things of no eternal consequence and fall for the sucker lies of the evil one that possessions and status are the means to fulfilment and self-worth.'[124]

The question is whether practical love and a high-consumption lifestyle are compatible – or whether, like the rich young ruler who met Jesus,[125] we must choose.

Elsewhere Guillebaud writes:
'What's it worth to follow Jesus? How far is too far when he stretched out his arms on the cross and went that far? Do you want the adventure of living, or would you prefer the safety of existing? Aren't you itching for a deeper and more raw expression of following Jesus? Aren't we meant to be dangerous people, wide-eyed radicals, dreamers of the day? What does radical living look like in the 21st century? Or shall I just resign myself to a safe, sanitised, respectable middle-class Christianity?'[126]

124   Simon Guillebaud, Dangerously Alive: An African Adventure of Faith Under Fire, Oxford: Monarch, 2011

125   Mark 10:17-27

126   Simon Guillebaud, Dangerously Alive: An African Adventure of Faith Under Fire, Oxford: Monarch, 2011

YOUR PAIN IS MY PAIN

The biblical injunction to love others 'as you love yourself'[127] points to the final, decisive characteristic of Christ-like love: compassion. The word compassion has its root in two Latin ideas - 'com' meaning the same as (think 'companion' - the one who shares the same bread as me) and passion meaning suffering (as in 'the passion of Christ'). To have compassion is not merely to feel pity, or to be stirred to help. It is to share suffering; to make your pain my pain. At its root the word kindness has the same meaning - I treat you well because we are 'of the same kind'.

The radical, revolutionary message of Jesus is that this 'sameness' applies to all humanity. It is not only to my own family, or tribe, or nation, or race that I owe compassion, but to all those I meet. When Jesus was asked to define 'neighbour,' he told a story not about ethnicity or tribe but about a stranger accidentally encountered.[128] My neighbour is the one I stumble across who is in need. More significantly still, the stranger's status is changed by my choice to be a neighbour to them.[129] The only limit on the love I am able to offer is my choice. My neighbour – the one I am asked by Scripture to love as I love myself - is defined by who I choose to love.

Religious Leader: But who is my neighbour?
Jesus: Everyone you choose to love. Everyone you come across and choose not to ignore. Everyone God sends you. Everyone.

The significance of Jesus' answer is not only in who it includes, but in who it does not exclude. The leader asks 'Who is my neighbour?' but what he really means is 'Who is not? Who can I afford not to love?' 'Who can I leave off my love-list?' 'Who can I exclude and ignore?' But Jesus will not allow this, so he answers in such a way as to exclude no-one. There is no-one who is not your neighbour, your family; your kind. All are included – you choose how far to go in expressing this.

Practical love, after the model of Jesus, is a challenging and transforming choice.

127   Matthew 22:34-40

128   The Parable of the Good Samaritan, Luke 10:25-37

129   Luke 10:36

• • •

ENCOUNTERING GOOD NEWS:

JESSIE JOE JACOBS

'And how can they call on the one they have not believed, and how can they believe if they have never been told and how can they be told if they have never been sent?'[130]

I often describe that moment I gave God everything as being as if I was on a running machine and suddenly someone just picked me up and put me on the open road. All the stuff I had held on to, the status with my job, the partying and drinking and socialising, suddenly it was no longer important anymore. The things I had struggled the most to give up, I was no longer interested in.

I didn't want to get drunk anymore; I wasn't interested in crazy nights out or drinking into the early hours. I used to swear like a trooper and suddenly flip became the worst expletive I could get out my mouth. Also I didn't feel empty anymore or bored. I was just so full of love and life. I could hardly contain what I was feeling. I just felt free. I was so happy I was unable to contain it. It was like someone had given me some drug that never wore off. I was completely different.

I immediately wanted to go and tell EVERYONE. I think maybe because of the dark place my life had got to; when I chose to become a Christian, I was so astounded, so impacted and so excited about the incredible difference it was making in my life, about God's incredible love; I think I just wanted everyone to know.

I saw Stockton in new eyes; it was like it just seemed so obvious to me that if my life could have been so dramatically turned around, it could happen for all these other people who were trapped in dark places such as addiction, depression, loneliness etc. It wasn't long before this vision of what Stockton and its people could be became an increasing burden on my heart. I had a vision of a girl who was selling her body on the streets and it ruined me forever. A verse that stayed with me for a long time was this:

I knew I needed to be sent. I wanted to tell everyone that there was hope. That life could be different. That there was a God who loved them. My biggest burden was girls who were being sexually exploited and children addicted to drugs. I quit my job. I gave up a number of things and along with a handful of passionate women, we set up a ministry called A Way Out.[131] We began to go out on the streets and estates of Stockton sharing the love of God in practical ways. We helped women get into treatment for addiction. We educated young people about the dangers of drugs. We became a shoulder to cry on when someone was in need; a friend in a life of loneliness. We visited young people in hospital who had overdosed; became a birthing partner for a teenage mum; went to court with women addicted to crack and heroin; visited mums and sisters in prison. We became family to many who had lost their families through life's challenges. Ten years on, we estimate 5,000 people will have come into contact with an A Way OUT worker. We employ a team of 22 people. We have a bespoke designed outreach and support centre. We have just been given our first vehicle.

Sadly, we still have many challenges to overcome; as the team grows, so does the need. We are just seeing one life turned around when five new people arrive at our services looking for help but we wouldn't want to be anywhere else. We are being the good news one life at a time and it is the best possible place to be.[132]

---

130   Romans 10:14

131   'At-risk Women And Youth OUTreach' www.awayout.co.uk

132   Jessie Joe Jacobs is Chief Executive of A Way Out, www.awayout.co.uk

● ● ●

ENCOUNTERING GOOD NEWS: KATE COLEMAN

I was 18 years old when I first seriously 'encountered' Jesus. It was the most surprising moment of my life; however, NOT because I was without spiritual awareness. Living in Camden, London, meant I was no stranger to a variety of New Age ideologies or the power of spirituality. My encounter took everyone by surprise, including me, largely because most of the Christians I had known up until then lived a very different (and frankly boring) version of the gospel they preached, so I was thoroughly disinterested in the God they spoke about. Then I suddenly encountered Jesus not just as the source of life but also as the source of all truth. Even today, whenever I recall those Christians who effectively, put me off Jesus, I am reminded that Jesus seeks not only to work through us, but also in us. This means that the best sermon illustration we have at our disposal as Christians is the life we lead and the way we lead it.

Three years later, I was half way up a mountain in Scotland trying desperately to figure out what God wanted me to do with my life after university. While I was there, I encountered Jesus as the source of my calling. He called me to church leadership. This was also a huge surprise because my church didn't believe in women in leadership and, interestingly, neither did I. However, two years later I was leading that very same church. This was also a time of great sacrifice for me. I lost valued friends in the process of walking in obedience to that call. Thankfully, Jesus walked with me and continues to do so. Every Christian is called to make the ultimate sacrifice for Jesus; we usually equate this with a willingness to die for Jesus, I discovered that this meant being willing to live, sometimes uncomfortably, for Jesus.

Another major encounter occurred years later during a personal 'identity crisis'. What did it mean to be young, single, black and female in a context that was generally unsympathetic to all these distinctives? I still remember a young black Christian asking me, 'Does God hate black people?' I have to confess I was stumped, the evidence didn't look good. The popular media messages suggested that all black people lived in poverty, in conflict or simply didn't know how to govern themselves. It was a tough time for me. I began to pray and as I responded to Jesus' prompting to 'dig deeper,' I encountered Jesus as the source of my identity. The words, 'Study to show thyself approved unto God', took on a whole new meaning. I explored the black presence in the Bible and British history and unearthed the most amazing facts (much of which is now taught in schools and every October during black history month). I learned about Sojourner Truth, Mary Seacole and Olaudah Equiano.

I discovered that the first university in the world existed in Timbuktu and the first Bible college in Alexandria, both in Africa. I learned that the first black people arrived in Britain at least 500 years before the English themselves began living in England Thankfully, today I can point others to numerous black, single, female, Christian role models engaged in world-changing activities.

Jesus continues to be my source, not least of wonder and surprise![133]

SUMMARY

Lives shaped by the person and words of Jesus - who he is and what he says – will express themselves in the actions of Jesus. We will do the things he did and join with him in the things he is doing today. What does it mean for you for your actions to be marked by the love of Christ?

---

133   Rev Dr Kate Coleman chairs the Evangelical Alliance Council, is a former President of the Baptist Union of Great Britain, Associate Pastor of a church plant and Director of Next Leadership www.nextleadership.org

PROPHETIC: MAKING A DIFFERENCE

Just as we saw that our speaking can be both private and public - we communicate the good news in private words and public spaces - so too our actions can have both a personal and a corporate dimension. And just as our choice to love can make a difference to one person - one stranger encountered on the road - so our decisions to live a life shaped by the love of Christ can impact whole cultures. There are times when our love is not only practical but becomes prophetic: embodying the purposes of God and pointing the world towards its future. Paul speaks of the Holy Spirit as the deposit guaranteeing our future inheritance,[134] and it is through the Holy Spirit at work in us that we are able to take hold of the 'not yet' of God's kingdom and bring it into the 'now' of our experience.

BOARDING THE WRONG TRAIN

A remarkable 20th century example of prophetic action has been brought once again into the spotlight recently with the publication of a new biography of Dietrich Bonhoeffer. Eric Metaxas' Bonhoeffer: Pastor, Martyr, Prophet, Spy[135] throws new light on the important connection between Bonhoeffer's personal faith and his decision to stand against Hitler's regime.

Highlighting watershed moments in Bonhoeffer's journey, Mataxas writes:

'In April 1933, during the early months of Nazi rule in Germany, the 'Aryan Paragraph,' as it came to be called, went into effect. A new law banned anyone of Jewish descent from government employment. Hitler's assault on the Jews - already so evidently

under way in his toxic rhetoric and in the ideological imperatives of his party - was moving into a crushing legal phase. German churches, which relied on state support, now faced a choice: preserve their subsidies by dismissing their pastors and employees with Jewish blood—or resist. Most Protestant and Catholic leaders fell into line, visibly currying favour with the regime or quietly complying with its edict.

Such ready capitulation makes the views of Dietrich Bonhoeffer, a young Lutheran theologian in Hitler's Germany, all the more remarkable. Within days of the new law's promulgation, the 27-year-old pastor published an essay titled 'The church and the Jewish Question,' in which he challenged the legitimacy of a regime that contravened the tenets of Christianity. The churches of Germany, he wrote, shared 'an unconditional obligation' to help the victims of an unjust state 'even if they [the victims] do not belong to the Christian community'. He went further: Christians might be called upon not only to 'bandage the victims under the wheel' of oppression but 'to put a spoke in the wheel itself.' Before the decade was out, Bonhoeffer would join a conspiracy to assassinate Hitler and pay for such action with his life.'[136]

Bonhoeffer's initial stance is summed up in stark and simple words:

'...a church that was not willing to stand up for the Jews in its midst was not the real church of Jesus Christ.'[137]

This was not simply a political decision, nor even an application of some universal notion of justice. It was a theological commitment: a distinctive and specific outworking of the Jesus story. It was, Metaxas suggests, the direct fruit of Bonhoeffer's own encounter with the good news of Jesus:

---

134   Ephesians 1:14

135   Eric Metaxas, Bonhoeffer: Pastor, Martyr, Prophet, Spy, Thomas Nelson Publishers, 2011

136   Joseph Loconte, 'Belief in Action' Wall Street Journal, April 23rd 2010, online at http://online.wsj.com

137   Eric Metaxas, Bonhoeffer: Pastor, Martyr, Prophet, Spy, Nashville: Thomas Nelson, 2010

'He had theologically redefined the Christian life as something active, not reactive. It had nothing to do with avoiding sin or with merely talking or teaching or believing theological notions or principles or rules or tenets. It had everything to do with living one's whole life in obedience to God's call through action. It did not merely require a mind, but a body too. It was God's call to be fully human, to live as human beings obedient to the one who made us, which was the fulfilment of our destiny. It was not a cramped, compromised, circumspect life, but a life lived in a kind of wild, joyful, full-throated freedom - that was what it was to obey God...'[138]

Bonhoeffer's own account of the foundation from which his convictions grew is unambiguous:
'The Christian is the man who no longer seeks his salvation, his deliverance, his justification in himself, but in Jesus Christ alone. He knows that God's word in Jesus Christ pronounces him guilty, even when he does not feel his guilt, and God's word in Jesus Christ pronounces him not guilty and righteous, even when he does not feel that he is righteous at all.'[139]

But equally unambiguous is his recognition that this central commitment to Christ calls for a public stand against injustice that might at times be painful; that might involve the risking of one's very life.

Bonhoeffer wrote:
'There is no way to peace along the way of safety, for peace must be dared, it is itself the great venture and can never be safe. Peace is the opposite of security. To demand guarantees is to want to protect oneself. Peace means giving oneself completely to God's commandment, wanting no security, but in faith and obedience laying the destiny of the nations in the hand of Almighty God, not trying to direct it for selfish purposes. Battles are won, not with weapons, but with God. They are

won when the way leads to the cross.'[140]
Bonhoeffer was not persuaded to take a more moderate, or less controversial view by the fact that so many of his brothers and sisters in Christ had chosen to do so. Asked why he wouldn't join the German Christians in order 'to work against them from within,' he said:

'If you board the wrong train, 'it is no use running along the corridor in the opposite direction.'[141]

An earlier biography of Bonhoeffer confirms that this courageous, prophetic spirit continued to animate him to the very moment of his death:

His last weeks were spent with men and women of many nationalities; Russians, Englishmen, Frenchmen, Italians and Germans. One of these, an English officer, wrote:

'Bonhoeffer always seemed to me to spread an atmosphere of happiness and joy over the least incident and profound gratitude for the mere fact that he was alive. ... He was one of the very few persons I have ever met for whom God was real and always near. ...On Sunday, April 8, 1945, Pastor Bonhoeffer conducted a little service of worship and spoke to us in a way that went to the heart of all of us. He found just the right words to express the spirit of our imprisonment, the thoughts and resolutions it had brought us. He had hardly ended his last prayer when the door opened and two civilians entered. They said, "Prisoner Bonhoeffer, come with us." That had only one meaning for all prisoners - the gallows. We said good-bye to him. He took me aside: "This is the end, but for me it is the beginning of life." The next day he was hanged in Flossenburg.'[142]

138   Eric Metaxas, Bonhoeffer: Pastor, Martyr, Prophet, Spy, Nashville: Thomas Nelson, 2010

139   Dietrich Bonhoeffer, Life Together, San Francisco: Harper and Row, 1954

140   Eric Metaxas, Bonhoeffer: Pastor, Martyr, Prophet, Spy, Nashville: Thomas Nelson, 2010

141   Eric Metaxas, Bonhoeffer: Pastor, Martyr, Prophet, Spy, Nashville: Thomas Nelson, 2010

142   Dietrich Bonhoeffer, Life Together, San Francisco: Harper and Row, 1954

Bonhoeffer stands as a remarkable model of prophetic action for two particularly significant reasons:

- Because the stand he made was against a force that is now all but universally acknowledged as evil, but that at the time was accepted or acquitted by many of Christ's followers.

- Because as an accomplished theologian and skilled writer, he has left us an excellent and detailed record of the why of his actions.

The challenge for us in our own time is to discern, as Bonhoeffer did, the forces against which we are called to stand. What are the issues over which it is appropriate – even imperative - for Christians to risk their lives today? Does the choice to clearly identify Jesus as our source help us, in turn, to identify these issues? The dilemma faced by the Chapter of St Paul's Cathedral recently when the 'Occupy' movement took up residence, brought these choices starkly into the light for many believers. In a stand-off between the establishment and those protesting against it, where does the church stand? Where would Jesus be? This was, for many, a genuine dilemma - one that did not offer itself up to easy answers. Where else in our culture are such decisions buried? Where else might the call of the Holy Spirit to prophetic action be heard? 'A human being's moral integrity begins when he is prepared to sacrifice his life for his convictions,' Bonhoeffer wrote.[143] Over what issues might such a sacrifice be asked of us today? Are there lesser sacrifices, of comfort or reputation, that fall short of us giving our lives but call us, all the same, to risk a prophetic stand?

One important area to explore is the way we relate to a culture of 'therapeutic consumerism'[144] Ruth Valerio takes up the challenge.

//

143   Eric Metaxas, Bonhoeffer: Pastor, Martyr, Prophet, Spy, Nashville: Thomas Nelson, 2010

144   Walter Bruggemann

LIVING LIGHTLY: OPTIONS FOR A GOOD NEWS LIFESTYLE?[145]

Standing at the heart of the notion of being prophetic is the idea of living lives and speaking words that are at odds with the society around us. The Old Testament prophets were a mixed bunch of people – some of them were part of the religious structure of the nation (e.g. Ezekiel, who was a priest) whilst others were regular people with everyday jobs (e.g. Amos, who was a shepherd). But whoever they were, we know them for their forthright words (positive as well as negative: the job of a prophet is not simply to condemn) and for the things they did in their lives (think of Hosea marrying Gomer and Jeremiah's linen belt).

Not many of us will be called to be prophets in this strict sense of the term, but we are all called to be different to the culture that we are a part of. That does not mean being weird, but it does mean that we will not just take on board all the expectations and assumptions that are an integral part of how our society works. Christians through the ages have been faced with the challenge of working out how to live in the society that they're a part of whilst keeping hold of their identity in Christ, and that is no less true for us today, living in our consumer-focussed society.

Consumerism has brought us many benefits and we should beware being too naively 'anticonsumerist'.[146] Nonetheless, many of the values that underpin consumerism are very problematic and cause a lot of damage, and as followers of Jesus we should question how much a part of that we should be. Our consumer society is based on the basic rule that continual financial growth is good, and this is given a higher priority than looking after people or places. Governments, business and individuals; we all live by this basic rule. Why not take a few minutes to think through where you see that happening?

The result is that, at the same time as enjoying a higher standard of living than at any other time in human history, we are also facing the pressures of having to maintain that. So, many of us deal daily with lives that are stressed and tiring. We feel we do not have the time we would like to give to our friendships and our walk with God. We are bombarded with messages that tell us we need a better car, a bigger and warmer house, nicer clothes, no grey hair, the next technological gadget etc, and too often, despite our protestations, we fall for those messages and spend our energies and our money pursuing those things.

And all the time we do that we are unaware of the impact that our actions are having on people and the wider creation. A large part of the problem is that we are cut off from the effects of our consumer-based lifestyle as everything is presented to us abstracted.

We don't see the power station that fires up when we turn on the lights, or the chicken that has become meat in plastic, or the oil field that supplies the petrol for our car.

As William Cavanaugh says, we do not give these issues much thought, 'not necessarily because we are greedy and indifferent to the suffering of others, but largely because those others are invisible to us'.[147] In general, we don't make things anymore (so we're separated from material production), we don't know who has made our products (we are separated from the producers and the land they inhabit), and we are separated from the actual products themselves (as we move onto new things so quickly, whether through not knowing how to fix something or through upgrading).

145   Ruth Valerio

146   See the Breathe - short videos looking at different aspects of consumer culture at conspiracyoffreedom.org

147   William Cavanaugh, Being Consumed: Economics and Christian Desire, Eerdmans 2008

The negative impacts that our consumer society is having – on the wider creation, on ourselves and on other people, particularly those who are poor – go right against what God desires for his world: for flourishing and shalom, with no injustice or oppression. And so the onus is on us, as Jesus' followers, to find ways of living that pursue God's heart for justice and righteousness, right in the midst of our society. With the heavy impact that consumerism has, we must learn to live more lightly.[148]

Here are five suggestions:

1. Use your money in ways that encourage connection rather than separation.
E.g. Bank/invest with an ethical bank that tells you where your money is going to; shop locally so that you get to know the shop keepers; buy your food from people who were involved in that food's production; give to people and organisations with whom you can have some sort of a relationship; buy Fairtrade whenever that is an option.

2. Do things that connect you with how things are produced.
E.g. Learn how to mend your bike; grow some food; cook things from scratch; learn to sew; install renewable energy at home; turn your yoghurt pots into seedling containers; install a water butt; make your own bread.

3. Set intentional limits on your consumption.
E.g. Buy no new clothes for a year unless you absolutely need to; walk, cycle or use public transport rather than drive; learn to live in a colder house and turn the heating down; cut down on the amount of meat you eat; if offered an upgrade on your smart phone, turn it down and tell the company that you are happy with what you currently have; take a holiday without flying.

4. Give time to community and relationships.
E.g. Get involved in local community activities; join (or start) a community/residents' association; become informed on what decisions your local council are making and get involved in influencing them; give time and/or homemade presents; cook a meal for a busy friend or neighbour.

5. Get stuck into the issues of our world.
E.g. See what 350.org and Friends of the Earth are up to and get involved; sign up to Tearfund campaigns; subscribe to magazines such as The Ecologist, New Internationalist and Ethical Consumer to become more informed; keep up to date with the news and pray regularly.

148 www.arocha.org.uk/livinglightly

AGAINST THE ACCUSER

An important aspect of Jesus-led prophetic action is to know that it is not against people that we stand, but against the principalities and powers that are somehow operating behind, around and perhaps through them. It is against evil that we stand. The apostle John wrote succinctly that 'The reason the Son of God appeared was to destroy the devil's work.'[149]

Tom Wright leaves us in no doubt as to the centrality of this conflict with evil to Jesus' own sense of calling:

'In Jesus own understanding of the battle he was fighting, Rome was not the real enemy. Rome provided the great gale, and the distorted ambitions of Israel, the high-pressure system. But the real enemy, to be met head-on by the power and the love of God, was the anti-creation power, the power of death and destruction, the force of accusation, the Accuser who lays a charge against the whole human race and the world itself that all are corrupt and decaying, that all humans have contributed to this by their own idolatry and sin. The terrible thing is that this charge is true. All humans have indeed worshipped what is not divine and so have failed to reflect God's image into the world. They, and creation, are therefore subject to corruption and death. At this level the Accuser is absolutely right. But the Accuser is wrong to imagine that this is the creator's last word...'[150]

Several conclusions can be drawn for our own context from this assertion:

1. Whatever is against God, God is against. All those forces and structures in our culture that thwart the purposes of God, that prevent his human creatures from knowing and enjoying intimacy with him, are on the Son of God's demolition schedule.

2. It is always the will of God for the will of God to be done. Addiction, for example, is an evil force that distorts humanity and resists God's kingdom. Is it ever God's will for an addiction to remain unbroken? Is God ever 'for' addiction? Or can we safely say wherever human lives are blighted by addictions, God is against that force, and for their freedom? What about slavery? Pornography? Violence towards children?

3. Prophetic action begins in prayer. The link between prophetic action and the mission of Jesus to destroy evil is captured in the most basic of all Christian prayers - for the will of God to be done on earth as in heaven. As we pray for God's heart for the world, might we find ourselves drawn into action.

One way of using the Lord's Prayer as an aid in identifying the issues over which God's heart is broken is to take an issue and ask 'Do I believe this is happening in Heaven? If not, will I pray and work until it isn't happening on Earth?'

149   1 John 3:8 NIV

150   N T Wright, Simply Jesus: A New Vision Of Who He Was, What He Did, And Why it Matters, London: Harper Collins, 2011

EXERCISE: IDENTIFY YOUR PROPHETIC OPPORTUNITIES

What are the challenges facing you and your faith community in these early years of the 21st century? See if you can identify three issues in each of the following areas that are crying out for a Jesus-centred prophetic response:

1. In the PERSONAL sphere
- three things you may need to challenge.

2. In your LOCAL CONGREGATION
- three things you can, together, take on.

3. Across your CITY / AREA
- three things the Body of Christ, as a whole, should engage with.

4. GLOBALLY
- three things the gospel should be known for its stance on.
Now review your list of twelve issues or areas of action. What might be a first step for each
- in prayer or in action?

WORKING WITH OTHERS

The above exercise highlights the fact that whilst there are certain issues we can respond to personally, or as a particular congregation, there are others that require a more united approach. Can we change our default from working on our own to investing in strategic partnerships? What areas of concern are there in your city or area for which only a whole church response will be effective? What are the headline issues over which the whole church may be called to make a stand?

LOVING ALL CREATION

Also implicit in this approach is the assertion of God's love for all creation - the human and the non-human. Enlightenment thinking has bequeathed to us a radical separation between the human and the non-human aspects of God's creation. God loves and saves people, we assert, but merely 'watches over' animals and nature. This falls short of the Bible's full picture, where the love of God for the whole world - the very cosmos - stirs him to sacrifice his own son. Is there work for us to do in redressing this balance? Can we work out, in the context of a global environmental crisis, what it means for the words 'gospel' and 'kingdom' to have meaning - and give hope - to God's non-human creation?

```

## PROPHETIC ACTION: FAIRTRADE GOLD

In 2011, readers of the Guardian and Observer newspapers voted committed Christian Greg Valerio their 'Campaigner of the Year' for his work towards a Fairtrade certification for the world's gold trade. For Valerio, this marked the culmination of a lifetime's commitment to a faith that moves beyond the simple statement 'I believe in Jesus' call to embody Christ's love for the poor: a call he first responded to in the slums of Addis Ababa:

'My journey in jewellery has taken me to the cross roads of the most intense beauty, the most sublime craftsmanship imaginable, yet equally the most corrupting, conflict-soaked materials the human psyche can tolerate,' Greg writes. 'The road has been a divergent, spiritually eclectic discovery of the best and worst in humanity: the finest qualities rooted in the human spirit as indigenous people have cried out for justice in the face of the immoral practices of transnational mining companies; the worst of humanity, that

# we allow small-scale gold miners to suffer gruelling hours in the sun for a dollar a day and half a cup of rice,

to satisfy the rapacious appetites of international gold traders.

The endemic bonded slave and child labour that exists in the mines of Africa and South America to deliver gold and diamonds to wedding jewellery is perhaps one of our world's most intentional deceptions, as we exchange iconoclastic symbols of love and fidelity in the name of Christ that are sourced in such abject poverty and exploitation. The horror has been extreme and at times soul destroying and criminally nihilistic, when faced with the vast structural injustices that perpetuate exploitation in the name of glamour. In desiring to be a Fairtrade jeweller, I did not fully understand the extent to which I would be exposed to the warring factions of 'the love of God and love of mammon'.

So faith in Christ is not an abstract. The ethical purity of the Creator Trinity has forced me to draw on my Christ-centred convictions and to re-imagine a jewellery product that was not exploitative and corrupt. I had to imagine what a righteous wedding ring would look like. As I contemplated, over many years and through trial and tribulation, I came to understand that jewellery can be a powerfully redemptive product. It can harness the most beautiful of raw materials born of God, like gold, diamonds, rubies, sapphires. These materials are found in the most beautiful locations of our world: rain forests, deserts, savannahs and mountains.

They are anointed with the sweat of the small-scale miner whose dignity is rooted in the image of God, and they carry an intrinsic value both materially as well as aesthetically that can bring economic justice to the poor and restoration to the land. In the hands of a skilled artisan craftsman they can be forged, honed and reworked to create beauty that is endowed with emotional and aspirational power. In many ways this vision is eschatological.

As I meditated on some of the images of heaven recorded in Scripture I saw a new Jerusalem made from all precious stones and whose streets were made of gold as transparent as glass. This romantic vision of the harmony of creation climaxing in its truest form and purpose has given me great consolation when faced with the 'dark satanic souls and greed' of our modern-day, large-scale, cyanide-infested mining companies, whose purpose is not creational redemption, but profiteering at any price to the land and people.

The creation of Fairtrade Gold is perhaps the first step on a long road to the realising of a jewellery product that brings justice, beauty and dignity back to those that mine and fashion this most discretional and luxurious product.'[151]

151   Greg Valerio, Jeweller and Activist; Founder of CRED Jewellery and co-founder of Fair Jewellery Action for more see www.fairjewelry.org www.credjewellery.com
```

ENCOUNTERING GOOD NEWS: BEKAH LEGG

I've known Jesus all my life. I can't remember a time when I've not been aware of his presence in my life, not seen his hand guiding me, not known that he has great plans for me. It's an extraordinary gift to have always known him, but one I've sometimes taken for granted. There have been times when I have metaphorically put my hands over my ears and lalala'd God, not wanted to hear the guidance, not wanted to follow the plans, and some of those times took me to a place of complete crisis; a place where I felt trapped, literally, on the other side of the world, in an abusive marriage with a baby and another on the way.

I couldn't see a way out, I didn't know how to reach my hand back out to find the God who I knew was waiting for me; his own hand ready, his plans as good as they ever were. I didn't know how to look at the Jesus I felt I had let down so terribly. But Jesus met me in my crisis and in a story too long to tell here, he set me free with a verse from Zephaniah:

'Sing, Daughter Zion...Israel! Be glad and rejoice with all your heart, Daughter Jerusalem. The Lord has taken away your punishment, he has turned back your enemy. The Lord, the King of Israel, is with you; never again will you fear any harm... The Lord your God is with you, the Mighty Warrior who saves. He will take great delight in you; in his love he will no longer rebuke you, but will rejoice over you with singing.'[152]

For me, the good news of walking with Jesus has been freedom. Physical freedom, but also freedom from my past, freedom from the pain and the hurt and the lies. But better than that, it is a freedom to be; to be all that I was created to be, to step out of the past and into my future. With that freedom comes responsibility: because, although there are days when my past catches up with me again, my chains have actually been broken, but there are still millions of women around the world who live in bondage.

Nearly two years ago I began to edit Liberti magazine[153] and it has provided me with an opportunity to use my gifts to speak for those who can't do it for themselves; to raise awareness of women who are oppressed around the world, to elevate the debate about the equality of women in the church and to prompt, inspire and encourage women to dream big and live lives of freedom. Outside of that, as a family, we choose to give freedom to four children that we sponsor through Compassion – releasing them from poverty and enabling them to dream. We open our home to young people whose own homes are not safe places to be, giving them dinner and a listening ear and occasionally a bed for the night. I go into local schools running assemblies and workshops that tackle issues of boundaries and self-esteem, equipping young people with the tools they need to live free from the tyranny of society's expectations. You see, freedom is a wonderful thing, but it's made for sharing.[154]

---

152 Zephaniah 3:14-15,17

153 www.libertimagazine.com

154 Bekah Legg is the Editor of Liberti magazine and Education Co-ordinator at Lifecentre, an organisation supporting the survivors of sexual abuse. She is a youth worker at Arun Community Church, West Sussex.

SUMMARY

Proclaiming what is right and true and just in Christ may lead us to confront what is not right and true and just in our culture. Our commitment may challenge our culture. What might it mean for you to act prophetically in your cultural setting? What are the issues the good news is asking you to confront?

INTERLUDE

A poet, spiritual writer and Fellow of King's College, London, Evelyn Underhill was, in her day, one of Britain's most influential writers on prayer. In 1940 she published Abba: Mediations Based Upon The Lord's Prayer. Here is her explanation of how it is that the individual encounter with Christ and the inward journey it initiates becomes the outward journey to a world transformed:

'There will be two sides to this: passive and active. The passive side means enduring, indeed welcoming, the inexorable pressure of God's transforming power in our own lives; for the kingdom comes upon earth bit by bit, as first one soul and then another is subjugated by love and so redeemed. It means enduring the burning glance of the Holy, where that glance falls on imperfection, hardness, sin.

The active side means a self-offering for the purposes of the kingdom, here and now in this visible world of space and time; the whole drive of our life, all our natural endowments, set towards a furtherance of the purposes of God. Those purposes will not be fulfilled till the twist is taken out of experience, and everything on earth conforms to the pattern in heaven - that is to say, in the mind of God: wide-spreading love transfiguring the whole texture of life. Here we have a direct responsibility as regards our whole use of created things: money, time, position, the politics we support, the papers we read.

It is true that the most drastic social reform, the most complete dethronement of privilege, cannot of themselves bring the kingdom; for peace and joy in the Holy Spirit can only come to us by the free gift of the Transcendent. But at least these can clear the ground, prepare the highway of God; and here each act of love, each sacrifice, each conquest of prejudice, each generous impulse carried through into action counts: and each unloving gesture, hard judgement, pessimistic thought or utterance opposes the coming of the kingdom and falsifies the life of prayer.

The coming of the kingdom is perpetual. Again and again freshness, novelty, power from beyond the world, break in by unexpected paths, bringing unexpected change.... the real Christian is always a revolutionary, belongs to a new race, and has been given a new name and a new song.

... To look with real desire for the coming of the kingdom means crossing over to God's side; dedicating our powers, whatever they may be, to the triumph of his purposes.'[155]

Do you have some sense, in your own situation, of what it might mean to dedicate your powers - whatever they are - 'to the triumph of his purposes'? How would you view the call to Christian mission if you were to define it as the coming of the kingdom to the places it has not yet come to; the will of God being done in situations in which it currently is not?

ENDWORD - KINGDOM COME

As we end this journey back to our source; as we consider the identity, words and actions Christ calls us to today, will you join with us in speaking out the words given to us by Jesus, and used throughout the church? This new adaptation of the Lord's Prayer by Rebekah Long[156] captures our longing for the will of God to be done on earth. Will you pray it with us? (Over the page)

155   Evelyn Underhill, Abba: Meditations Based Upon The Lord's Prayer, London: Longmans, 1940

156   Rebekah Long, The Bless Network, www.blessnet.eu

THE LORD'S PRAYER

OUR FATHER WHO DWELLS
IN THE HEAVENS AND ON THE EARTH,
YOU ARE HOLY.
MAY HEAVEN BE A GREATER PRESENT REALITY
HERE ON EARTH,
AND MAY WE CHOOSE TO JOIN YOU
IN MAKING THAT HAPPEN.
PROVIDE US TODAY
WITH THE THINGS THAT YOU THINK WE NEED,
AND MAY WE NOT TAKE FOR GRANTED
THAT WHICH YOU HAVE ALREADY PROVIDED.
FORGIVE US WHEN WE DON'T LIVE AS YOU INTEND,

AND MAY WE BE READY TO FORGIVE OTHERS
WHEN THEY DON'T LIVE AS WE INTEND.

GUIDE US IN YOUR WISDOM
AWAY FROM THE THINGS THAT WOULD DISTORT US,

AND RESTORE THE PARTS IN US
THAT ARE ALREADY DISTORTED.
YOU ARE GOODNESS, BEAUTY AND TRUTH.
MAY YOUR LOVE RULE ALWAYS.
AMEN[157]

---

157   Available at http://blessnet.eu/resources/lords-prayer/